Joy
IN THE MIDST

A STUDY OF PHILIPPIANS

CARRIE GAUL

REVIVE OUR HEARTS
NILES, MICHIGAN

For Joyce

My Kindred Spirit

"To God be the glory,

Great things He hath done."

1 Samuel 12:22–24

Table of Contents

WEEK ONE: OVERVIEW 6

WEEK TWO: PHILIPPIANS 1 18

WEEK THREE: PHILIPPIANS 2 34

WEEK FOUR: PHILIPPIANS 2 54

WEEK FIVE: PHILIPPIANS 3 72

WEEK SIX: PHILIPPIANS 3 84

WEEK SEVEN: PHILIPPIANS 4 102

WEEK EIGHT: PHILIPPIANS 4 116

APPENDIX

PHILIPPIANS WORKSHEET i

PEOPLE IN PHILIPPIANS xvi

KEY WORDS xx

© 2008 by Carrie Gaul

Edited by Kim Gwin
Designed by Laura Shaffer

Published by *Revive Our Hearts*
P.O. Box 2000, Niles, MI 49120
www.ReviveOurHearts.com

ISBN: #978-1-934718-20-9

Printed in the United States of America

INTRODUCTION TO *Joy in the Midst*

What a wondrous gift awaits us as we read over the shoulders of the Philippian Christians during these next weeks. They had just received a long-awaited letter from their precious friend and the founder of their church, the apostle Paul.

Gratitude must have filled their hearts as they recalled the one who had first brought the gospel message to the European Continent . . . to Philippi . . . to *Gentiles* . . . to **them**. Their lives had never been the same. How they longed to see their spiritual father again. How they must have rejoiced as they held the parchment in their hands, eagerly anticipating the words of the one they so dearly loved!

As you read the Philippians' precious letter over these next weeks, imagine what it would be like for you to receive words of encouragement and exhortation from the heart of the one who first shared the gospel message with you. Have you had that blessing? Do you recall reading those precious words? Once . . . then again and again. Perhaps you quickly skimmed it and then slowly reread every word, letting them sink deeply into your heart.

The letter you are about to read held that same depth of meaning for the Philippian believers.

Before you begin, please **take time to pray** and thank God for your spiritual father or mother—the person responsible for sharing the truth of the gospel with you. (You may even want to write them a short note expressing your gratitude.) Then ask God to open your heart to understand the truths of His Word as you begin this study of Philippians.

May your heart be filled with renewed passion for the gospel, your soul be consumed with the desire to know Jesus more intimately, and your life powerfully proclaim the message of "Joy in the Midst" . . . regardless of the circumstances.

Abundantly grateful for you,

Carrie

Day One
GAINING THE BIG PICTURE

We'll begin our study this week by reading through all four chapters of Philippians as we seek to gain a big-picture overview of this personal letter from Paul to the believers at Philippi. We've provided **Philippians Worksheets** in the appendix; feel free to make any markings on these. Take your time; this is the bulk of your assignment for today. Remember: This is not only Paul's letter to the Philippians, it's God's letter to *you*. What treasure does He want *you* to discover today?

As you read through Philippians, make a list of your **First Impressions** on page 16. Here are some questions to help you get started:

- What seems to have prompted Paul to write this letter?

- Where is Paul as he is writing?

- What is Paul's general tone? Is he instructing, encouraging, admonishing, warning, or correcting the Philippians?

- Is there a specific emphasis Paul seems to develop in this epistle?

- What type of relationship do you think Paul had with these believers? Why?

- What insights/truths about Paul or the Philippians stood out to you?

Have you sensed the hope and encouragement Paul has tucked into this short letter? The Philippians held a special place in Paul's heart; he was a spiritual father to many of them, and he understood the value of praise and thanksgiving. We see that evidenced throughout his letter.

Perhaps that's one reason Philippians is often called the "Epistle of Joy." A heart filled with gratitude and praise is also a heart overflowing with joy.

Think for a moment of an individual you've had the privilege of leading to the Lord. Consider taking a moment to write them a short note of encouragement and hope today. You may never know the full impact or the timeliness of your words.

Personal Take-Aways

At the end of each day, we will provide space for you to record any personal take-aways God may have shown you as you studied His Word. We want God to transform our lives—our thoughts, responses, and relationships—as we study His Word! So take some time to record how He has spoken to you. If you need help getting started, consider these questions about what you've just read.

How is God (Jesus/Holy Spirit) portrayed in this segment?

What truth from what you've read applies to your life today?

What steps of faith and/or action do you need to take to align your life with what you've seen?

What questions do you have about what you've read?

Day Two
THE APOSTLE PAUL

As we continue gaining a big picture of Philippians, we're going to learn all we can today about the author of this letter, the apostle Paul. As we do, allow these questions to continually run through your mind: How do I see my own life reflected in the life of Paul? How are Paul's thoughts, responses, and relationships similar to my own? How are they different?

Be sure to have your colored pencils ready!

Once again, read through Philippians on the **Philippians Worksheets**. (Yes, we know it has *four* chapters, and we are *so* proud of you for persevering!) This time as you read, mark in a distinctive way every reference to Paul (including personal pronouns).

Now take those beautifully colored pages and compile a list of facts on your **People in Philippians** chart found in the appendix. The facts you include on the list will answer specific questions concerning Paul; we call them "The 5 Ws and an H" (Who, What, When, Where, Why, How).

You will not necessarily write a fact for every mention of Paul's name; only record the obvious information that will answer one of those questions. Be sure to use words directly from the text. For example:

- Who is the author?

- Where is he?

- What are his circumstances?

- What is his attitude toward his circumstances?

- What does he say he does?

- What is his background?

For Our Zealous Friends

If you have extra time today, read these passages that give additional insights on Paul's life: Acts 7:58–8:3; 9; 11:19–26; 2 Corinthians 11:25–33; 12:7–10. Record any additional information on a separate sheet of paper.

Personal Take-Aways

If you were introducing Paul to a group of people who had never seen or heard of him, how would you describe this one who says, "To live is Christ and to die is gain"?

"It's my pleasure to introduce to you Paul, a man . . ."

As you've considered Paul's life, how is your life similar to his? How is it different?

Charles Spurgeon observed that "Scripture frequently sums up a man's life in a single sentence." How would you summarize Paul's life in one sentence?

If you were to die today, how might those who knew you best summarize your life in one sentence?

Day Three
THE BELOVED PHILIPPIANS

You guessed it—we're reading through Philippians once again. Our focus today will be on the recipients of this letter, the Philippian believers.

On your **Philippians Worksheet**, mark in a distinct way every reference to the Philippians (including pronouns and synonyms).

Now list the facts you've seen about the Philippians on your **People in Philippians** chart. Remember, only record the obvious information that answers the 5 Ws and an H questions, and use words directly from the text. For example:

- Who are the Philippians?

- Where are they?

- How are they described?

- What are their circumstances?

Based on what you've read, summarize what you've learned about those in the church at Philippi. What is taking place in their lives? In their church? What is life like for them in Philippi?

Do you ever look at other Christians and wish you knew the details of how God opened the truth of His gospel to them? I never tire of hearing those amazing stories.

When I was growing up, our church had regular Sunday evening services involving different activities, but my favorite was always testimony night—that time set aside to hear personal testimonies of God at work in people's lives. Periodically, a new believer would stand to testify of how God had brought a Christian friend across their path and used them to bring the hope of the gospel into their life.

Oh, how I loved those stories—because whatever the details, it was always a story of *amazing grace*!

For Our Zealous Friends

The believers at Philippi had just such a story of amazing grace. Before we end today, let's look at the details of their story. **Read Acts 16 and fill in the following blanks**:

On two separate occasions, Paul was prevented from entering an area where he would have preached the gospel. Rather, God gave Paul a vision to take the gospel into _____ (vv. 9–10). This would mark the first time the gospel was proclaimed on the _____ continent.

Paul and his traveling team settled for a time in _____, where _____ became the first convert in Europe. Following her conversion (and that of her household), Paul and Silas ran into some conflict that landed them in a Philippian _____ cell, where God had already begun preparing the heart of the _____ to receive the gospel. He then shared the wonder of the gospel with his family, who were also converted. So he began the first church at Philippi. *Amazing grace*!

Personal Take-Aways

What are the details of *your* story of God's amazing grace as He opened your eyes to the truth of the gospel? C. J. Mahaney, in *The Cross-Centered Life*, says we must never forget what we once were and what we are now. Only in this way will we remember the great mercy shown to us in Christ.

If you have a personal relationship with Jesus Christ, take a few minutes to remember who you were before you knew Christ, and who you are today. Record at least a summary of the details of God's amazing grace extended to you. Then spend time thanking Him for all He has done in bringing you out of darkness into His marvelous light!

Day Four
AN ATTITUDE OF REJOICING

By now you're becoming very familiar with this great letter to the Philippians. You've probably noticed several words repeated throughout the letter. These **key words** are used by Paul to convey his message to the Philippian believers.

Your assignment today is to read all four chapters, marking several of these **key words** in a distinctive way on your **Philippians Worksheet**. Then record the answers to the 5 Ws and an H questions on the **Key Words chart** found in the appendix.

- Joy/Rejoice

- Mind/Attitude

Are you surprised by Paul's attitude of joy in this letter? What does Paul say (or imply) brings him joy or causes him to rejoice?

Based on what you know of Paul, what reasons might he have had for not rejoicing?

Personal Take-Aways

Jesus said in John 15:11 that it is possible to have the fullness of His joy living in us, *right now*, in the midst of whatever our circumstances, whatever level of stress is threatening to undo us, whatever relational difficulties are tainting the canvas of our lives. Jesus said we can have His joy in the midst! "These things I have spoken to you so that My joy may be in you, and your joy may be made full" (John 15:11).

Amazing, isn't it? Yet we see it exemplified in Paul's life as we read his letter to the Philippians. Remember, we said this is more than just a personal letter to the Philippians; it's also God's personal letter to *you*. **What is He saying to you today in regard to rejoicing?**

In your daily life, how is God teaching you the truth of Nehemiah 8:10, "The joy of the LORD is your strength"?

THE LORD JESUS

You will rejoice with great rejoicing at the end of today—it's our last day of getting the big picture of Philippians! Next week we'll settle into chapter one for the whole week. But for today we're going to read all of Philippians one last time as we look for one more **key word**.

You are establishing a rich foundation as you immerse your heart and mind in the truths of God's Word. There is no greater use of your time, dear friend! Persevere in your study. Pray that God will enable you to apply the truths you are learning.

Have you noticed how often Paul refers to Christ in this short little thank-you note? There's a host of doctrinal truth concerning Christ's deity and lordship in this letter.

Today we want to mark every occurrence of the word *Jesus* (Christ, Lord, etc.) in a distinctive way. (Many people use a yellow pencil and make a cross through the middle of the word.)

After marking the text, make a list on your **Key Words chart** answering the 5 Ws and an H questions concerning Jesus.

You've had a full week of soaking in Philippians. You've learned a lot about the Philippians and their spiritual father, the great apostle Paul.

Based on what you've seen so far, what do you think Paul meant when he said in Philippians 1:21, "For to me, to live is Christ and to die is gain"?

Personal Take-Aways

Paul's life seemed to be consumed with one thing: Jesus Christ—His gospel, His cross, His love, His mercy—the One who had so dramatically changed Paul's life.

In a sentence or two, summarize the essence of what consumes your life.

Everyday life can often distract us from the truly important things—Jesus and His gospel. Although Paul's life was centrally focused on Christ, he too faced the reality of everyday life. Even in prison, Paul would probably have had responsibilities that could have become distractions for him.

In the midst of your everyday life, what practical steps have helped you keep Christ and the message of the gospel at the center of your life?

Are there steps you need to take to refocus your life? What are they? Will you prayerfully commit to engaging in this battle to keep Christ and the gospel at the center of your life? Take time to write out your commitment to the Lord.

First Impressions

- Paul wrote Philippians to correct, encourage, & instruct the Philippian church because they were introduced to the ~~the~~ rising threat of Judaizing
- Paul was in prison (1:14)
- He's encouraging & instructing
-

Notes

Day One
THE GOSPEL

Philippians Chapter One

We rejoiced last week as we recalled the day Christ first redeemed us from our sin, the day we were set free from darkness and brought into His marvelous light. What an incredible day! May we never lose the wonder of all that was accomplished on that old, rugged cross.

For many people those first days of wonder and amazement are followed by days of uncertainty and questions that can overshadow their initial zeal and wonder. Questions like, "Where do I go from here? What does God expect of me now that I'm a Christian? What can I expect from Him? How does a daughter of the King of Kings think, act, and relate to others?" So many questions. Where will they go for answers? Where do *you* go?

God did not save us from our sin and then leave us to figure out life on our own. His Word is saturated with truth—truth we desperately need, not only to be saved but to walk victoriously as His children. "For whatever is born of God is victorious over the world; and this is the victory that conquers the world, even our faith" (1 John 5:4 AMP).

This week, we'll look at life on the other side of the cross as we consider how to apply the gospel to everyday life. We so appreciate your commitment to be a student of the Word. We pray today that God would give you His wisdom and understanding as you seek to apply His truth to your life. "To You, O God of my fathers, I give thanks and praise, for You have given me wisdom and power; even now You have made known to me what we requested of You" (Dan. 2:23).

We'll begin today by reading through chapter one of Philippians and marking distinctively two key words in this particular chapter. See what you discover about the words *gospel* and *imprisonment*; then record what you learned on the **Key Words chart** from week one. As you record your findings, remember to use words directly from the text.

Paul was in a physical prison. Many Christians today also live in prisons; some are physical, some are not. **What prisons might some believers in this country be living in?**

The gospel was Paul's life. Wherever he went, whatever he did, the cross was the centerpiece of his teaching. He defended it, confirmed it, shared it boldly, and suffered for it repeatedly. In Acts 20:24 (NIV), Paul says, "I consider my life worth nothing to me, if only I may finish the race and complete the task the Lord Jesus has given me—the task of testifying to the gospel of God's grace." Because Paul *understood* the gospel, he could experience the *joy* of the gospel in the midst of hardship and persecution.

Take a few minutes to record the gospel message as you would describe it to one who has never heard the good news. Record any Scriptures you would use to substantiate the gospel truths.

In light of what you've outlined above, would you say that the gospel message is primarily for the unsaved or the saved individual? Explain.

Paul tucks numerous gospel truths into his letter to the Philippian believers. (We'll only look at those in chapter one for today.) These truths must have given them great hope. They must have rejoiced as they recalled all that was theirs as bondservants and saints of God Most High.

See if you can identify the gospel truths in the verses listed below. How does Paul describe the things that are true of us who are in Christ? Below the Scripture, record how your daily life might be impacted if you were to preach this gospel truth to yourself every day. It may help you to think in light of these statements: "Reminding myself of this truth would help me to . . ." or "would help me not to . . ." We've given some examples to get you started.

1:1 – I am a bondservant of Christ Jesus; I am a saint in Christ.

- *Reminding myself of this truth (bondservant) would help me be obedient and submissive to Christ, surrendering all my rights to Him.*

- *Reminding myself of this truth (sainthood) would give me purpose in life— I am called, I am set apart. God has a plan for me.*

1:6 – God will perfect the work He has begun in my life.

- *Reminding myself of this truth would help me not get discouraged when I repeatedly struggle with the same sin in my life.*

- *Reminding myself of this truth would help me have hope that God has not given up on those who are His but walking in rebellion toward Him.*

1:9 – God can cause my love for Him and others to abound (overflow).

-

-

1:9 – God will teach me knowledge and discernment as I love Him and others.

-

-

1:10 – As I grow, I will be able to distinguish what things are of greatest value.

-

-

1:10 – I can then stand sincere and blameless before Christ when He returns.

-

-

Now it's your turn. Record the gospel truths and how they might impact your life for each of the following verses.

1:11 – _____

     •

     •

1:12 – _____

     •

     •

1:28 – _____

     •

     •

1:29 – _____

     •

     •

Personal Take-Aways

Jerry Bridges said, "The gospel is not only the most important message in all of history; it is the only essential message in all of history. Yet we allow thousands of professing Christians to live their entire lives without clearly understanding it and experiencing the joy of living by it." [1]

Do you agree or disagree with his statement? If you agree, how do you see our lives individually and corporately being affected by a lack of understanding or living the gospel? If you disagree, what evidence do you see (either individually or corporately) that we *are* living our daily lives as Christians in light of the gospel?

Day Two
BONDSERVANTS AND SAINTS

Paul uses two very descriptive words in chapter one to help us understand what life looks like for each of us on the other side of the cross. He refers to himself and Timothy as *bondservants* of Christ, and to the Philippians as *saints* in Christ.

We're going to spend today looking at the meaning behind those words and how they apply to our lives. May God give us ears to hear, eyes to see, and hearts willing to obey. Don't forget to pray before you begin. May the Lord open our hearts to respond to His truth (Acts 16:14).

The Greek word for bondservant is transliterated (big word, simple meaning: a Greek word that has been written in English letters) *doulos*. Deuteronomy gives us the picture of a bondservant as one who, having served six years as a slave, chose to remain enslaved to his master rather than be set free. A *doulos* was one who was in a permanent relationship of servitude—his life altogether consumed in the will of another. For a clearer understanding of what is involved in being a bondservant, read Deuteronomy 15:12–18 and answer the following questions.

• Why would someone want to be a bondservant?

• How long was one to remain a bondservant?

• How was a bondservant marked? Read Galatians 6:17 and note how Paul was marked.

In Bible times, three classes of people wore brands: slaves, soldiers, and servants of temples. But what does that have to do with a Christian? **Look up the following Scriptures and record the class of people to which they refer. Also list how these verses relate to you as a Christian.** [2]

• 1 Corinthians 3:16–17

• 1 Corinthians 7:21–23

• 2 Timothy 2:3–4

Read the following Scriptures and see how they relate to being a bondservant. Record any new insights you gain into the life of a *doulos*.

• Matthew 10:24–25

• 1 Corinthians 6:19–20

• Galatians 1:10

Paul uses the word *saints* to describe the Philippian believers. **If you have a concordance and an expository dictionary, look up *saint* and see what you find before reading any further.** (If you don't have the tools, don't worry—we've got you covered! Keep reading . . .)

The Greek transliteration of the word saint is *hagios*. It means "holy, set apart, sanctified, consecrated." Saints are individuals set apart to God, consecrated to God's purposes. **Look up the following Scriptures and summarize what you learn about this holy life we are called to.**

• Exodus 19:3–6

• Leviticus 20:22–26

• 2 Corinthians 6:14–7:1

• 1 Peter 1:13–16; 2:9

Personal Take-Aways

Well, fellow bondservant and saint, you have definitely had a full day of study! We are so proud of you for pressing on, in the midst of *life* and all that involves. Thank you for your diligence. It does not go unnoticed by your heavenly Father.

Please don't leave your time in the Word today without asking God to help you personalize what you've learned. **How does He want you to apply the truths of what it means to be a saint who is set apart for Him, a bondservant whose life is solely consumed with his Master? Ask Him—He promises to answer you!**

"Before they call, I will answer; and while they are still speaking, I will hear" (Isa. 65:24).

Days Three and Four
LIFE AFTER DEATH

As you've read his letter, does it surprise you that Paul seems to be looking forward to death? In Philippians 1:21 he said that to die is gain. As he pens this letter to his beloved friends in Philippi, he is certainly realistic about the possibility of his death.

Yet death didn't seem to hold any fear for Paul. In fact, you can almost sense a longing for it! What about you? **When was the last time you seriously considered the certainty of your own death? What thoughts and feelings come to mind as you think of it? Take a moment to jot down your thoughts.**

If someone asked you, "What happens after we die?" how would you respond? We're going to focus on that question today as we consider what happens after death, both to those who know Christ as Savior and to those who do not. These are vital truths. May the understanding of these Scriptures deepen our anticipation and longing for heaven, and serve as a wake-up call as we think of friends and loved ones who do not yet know Christ.

We've got a lot of ground to cover; *please* don't forget to pray and ask God to give you an economy of time today as you dig into His Word. Also note that this lesson covers two days, so don't feel you have to rush through it.

Christ was the firstborn from among the dead to enter heaven. Christ's entry into heaven made it possible for a Christian's spirit and soul to enter heaven at death. **From Philippians 1, why do you think Paul so eagerly anticipated death?**

Read the following Scriptures and record what happens to a Christian's soul and spirit once he dies.

- 2 Corinthians 5:6–8

- Philippians 1:21–23

- 1 Thessalonians 4:13–18

Have you joined Paul in *longing* to depart and be with Christ? **Summarize below how you would convey to a friend the details of what happens to a Christian after they die. Be sure to include what *doesn't* happen.**

That, dear friends, is the *good* news. Now we must look into the rest of the story. What happens to those who are not Christ followers after they die? As you read, allow God to personalize these truths in your mind as you think of family members and friends who are unsaved.

The account of Lazarus and the rich man in Luke 16:19–31 takes place before the death and resurrection of Jesus. (If you are using the KJV, the word translated *hell* is more correctly translated *Hades*).

Draw a diagram of the information found in vv. 22–26.

Hades is a temporary holding place for non-believers until the Great White Throne judgment. After that judgment, all non-Christians will be cast into the lake of fire. This truth is taught in Revelation 20:11–15. **Read this passage and note what you learn.**[3]

In some places in the New Testament, *gehenna* has been translated "hell." The following passages all refer to *gehenna* or the lake of fire rather than Sheol or Hades. **Look up these references and record what you learn about the lake of fire.**[4]

- Matthew 10:28

- Matthew 25:41

- Mark 9:43

- Revelation 19:20

Following Christ is, indeed, a matter of life and death. Summarize the truths you have learned concerning those who die apart from Christ. Allow these truths to penetrate the very core of your being.

Personal Take-Aways

Have you been sobered by the reality of what awaits those who die apart from Christ? If you died tonight, do you know where *you* would spend eternity? If you have never repented of your sin and asked Jesus to be the Lord and Master of your heart, there is no better time than the present. Why not surrender to Him now?

If you have just prayed and received Christ as Lord and Savior, please let us know. We would love to pray for you in the days ahead.

Write out a prayer thanking God for what awaits you on the other side of eternity because of the gospel—Christ's work on the cross. Then ask Him to open the hearts and minds of those you love who will be in a Christless eternity if they were to die today.

Day Five
LIVING WORTHY OF THE GOSPEL

"So teach us to number our days that we may get a heart of wisdom" (Ps. 90:12 ESV). Matthew Henry said, "It ought to be the business of every day to prepare for our final day." As you have read and reread Paul's letter, do you get the impression he was always thinking of that final day?

Paul seemed to live his life from the perspective of the grave. He understood that what happens here on earth impacts all eternity. That understanding caused Paul to live a life worthy of the gospel. He instructs the Philippians to do the same. "Conduct yourselves in a manner worthy of the gospel of Christ" (Phil. 1:27). How do we do that? What does it look like to live in a manner worthy of the gospel of Christ?

Before we search for those answers, let's begin by gaining a "gravesite" perspective. Psalm 90:10 says the days of our life number 70 years, or at best 80. We'll use the best-case scenario! If God allows you to live 80 years, you will spend a grand total of 29,200 days on earth before stepping into eternity. Based on those figures, how much living have you already done? How much do you have left to go?

Multiply your age by 365 days. Then subtract that figure from 29,200. (If you really like math, you can also subtract the months since your last birthday).

How many days of your life have already passed?

If you were to be given 80 years on earth, how many days do you have left?

Sobering, isn't it? Someone once said that the most damaging aspect of contemporary living is short-term thinking. Can you relate? Isn't it easy to forget that life is far more than just here and now? Our time on earth is only a miniscule dot on the timeline of all eternity.

But it's a dot that has eternal significance. "For this reason," as the writer of Hebrews says, "we must pay much closer attention to what we have heard, so that we do not drift away from it. For . . . how will we escape if we neglect so great a salvation?" (Hebrews 2:1–3).

Let's look at Philippians 1:27–28 as we seek to define what it means to conduct ourselves in a manner worthy of the gospel.

What three marks does Paul use to describe those who are living worthy of the gospel?

Look up the following Scriptures and record any insights you gain about standing firm.

      • 2 Corinthians 1:24

      • Galatians 5:1

      • 2 Thessalonians 2:15

Reflect for a moment on what causes you to waver in your faith. When is it hardest for you to stand firm? What helps you stand firm?

Although there are certainly times when we are called on to stand alone for the gospel, God has designed the body of believers to work *together* in spreading the gospel. In fact, this is one of the ways we can live worthy of the gospel—by striving together with one purpose, one mind.

The word Paul uses for *striving* in verse 27 is *sunathleo*. It contains the word *athleo*, from which we get the word *athlete*. In the Scriptures, that same word has been translated "strive," "labor," and "compete" (Phil. 1:27; 4:3; 2 Tim. 2:5).

Reflect on the words *strive, athlete, labor,* **and** *compete.* **How do they help you understand what it means to live worthy of the gospel?**

How do you respond to the word *conflict*? Many of us start wavering when we are opposed or faced with hostility from those who set themselves against us as enemies. **If you've faced opposition for the gospel, describe the situation and your response below. Were you alarmed by it? What was it that caused you to be alarmed? Why do you think Paul tells the Philippians** *not* **to be alarmed?**

Personal Take-Aways

It's been a full week! We've covered a lot of ground as we've evaluated what it means to live as a daughter of the King of Kings. What has God shown you? How has He been speaking to your heart? What steps do you need to take in response to Him? Be sure to record what God is telling you. Take time to pray; don't just talk . . . listen.

"Speak, LORD, for Your servant is listening" (1 Sam. 3:9).

Notes

Day One
ATTITUDES, ATTITUDES, ATTITUDES!

Attitude: A little thing that makes a big difference. If you've spent more than 30 seconds on this planet, you know the reality of that statement! You've experienced it in your own life and in the lives of those you live and work with.

Attitudes are inward feelings and thoughts that are eventually expressed by outward behavior. Our attitudes are translated daily into actions and reactions for all the world (or at least all those who cross our path) to see. Unfortunately, our attitudes are often visible even in silence.

As you read through chapter two of Philippians, record any attitudes you see that may have existed in the Philippian church. Be sure to include the reference where you see evidence of each attitude.

Now look back at the attitudes you've discovered. Are any of these evident in your own life? Do you struggle with any of these same thoughts and feelings? Take a few minutes to reflect on the attitudes that most often rear their ugly heads in your life. List them below. What circumstances has God allowed recently that have evidenced these attitudes in your life?

Reread chapters 1, 3, and 4, looking for additional indications of external behavior that could reveal the Philippians' internal attitudes. **Add these to your list above.**

Our inward attitudes are often revealed as we bump into other people. These relational interactions shed light on attitudes we may wish to keep concealed. As we study Paul's letter to the Philippians, we'll see his deep love and concern for these fellow bondservants as he instructs them concerning specific attitudes.

Read through chapter two once again and record all the instructions Paul gave the Philippian Christians, along with the reference. Record these in one of the following columns:

DO   # DO NOT

Personal Take-Aways

As you consider Paul's instructions, remember that this is God's personal letter to you as well. Ask Him to show you one or two of these instructions that specifically fit a current situation in your own life. How can you mirror the attitude of Christ in that situation? What would Jesus do in the situation you just described? How would He act? What would He say?

Write out your own personal application for one of the instructions you listed above. Be specific: What do *you* need to do or not do? What do you need to believe or not believe? *Will you?* Write out your commitment.

Day Two

WHY DO I DO THE THINGS I DO?

"I don't understand why I act the way I do. I don't do what I know is right. I do the things I hate. Although I don't do what I know is right, I agree that the Law is good" (Rom. 7:15–16 CEV). Can you relate? Have you had days when you needed a retract button for your words or actions? Have there been times when your "dead" flesh seemed to rise from the grave, taking your thoughts and actions captive and leaving a path of pain and destruction in its wake?

You're not alone! It was the great apostle Paul who said, "I know the law but still can't keep it, and if the power of sin within me keeps sabotaging my best intentions, I obviously need help! I realize that I don't have what it takes. I can will it, but I can't do it. I decide to do good, but I don't really do it; I decide not to do bad, but then I do it anyway. My decisions, such as they are, don't result in actions" (Rom. 7:17–20 The Message).

Why do we—those who have been set free from the power of sin, indwelt by the Holy Spirit, and given everything we need for life and godliness—still struggle so desperately to exhibit Christ's attitude in our daily lives?

We're going to consider that question today in light of Philippians 2. But first, stop and ask the Lord to give you understanding related to this battle between your selfish desires and the humility that comes through Christ. "He gives wisdom to the wise and knowledge to the discerning. He reveals deep and hidden things; he knows what lies in darkness, and light dwells with him" (Dan. 2:21–22 NIV).

Begin your study today by reading Philippians 2 aloud. (If you are zealous, read all of Philippians aloud.) As you read, remember that the Philippians (a church originally comprised of all new believers) had been physically separated from Paul for at least 8 years (some scholars say as many as 10–12 years).

What do you think might have motivated Paul to include the content of Philippians 2:1–2 in his letter? Based on what he says, describe the condition the believers in Philippi may have been in spiritually, emotionally, relationally, and mentally.

Can you imagine how desperately these dear people must have needed Paul's encouragement, comfort, and fellowship? These are vital components to every believer's growth; God has designed us that way. Think about your life—not how it once was or even how you hope it will be one day, but the reality of what it is today. Then answer the following questions as honestly as possible.

- From whom or what do you seek encouragement? When the vise-grips of life squeeze you, where do you turn for comfort and support? Is it a person, an activity, a thing?

- Where do you turn for companionship, fellowship, camaraderie, friendship?

Praise God if He has provided you with those who will encourage and challenge you in the faith. Their encouragement is evidence that Christ is working in and through them as He desires to do.

But what if you are in a new place where you've not yet developed those types of relationships? Or what if you're married to an unbeliever who does nothing to encourage you in your walk with Christ? Or what if, because of persecution, you are one day separated from those who consistently build you up in the faith? What happens then? How will you survive?

Reread Philippians 2:1. Commentator Adam Clarke states the following: "The [Greek word translated] *if* does not express any *doubt* here, but on the contrary is to be considered as a *strong affirmation*." [5]

Based on this, what is Paul is saying in verse 1? Where will we always find encouragement, comfort, and fellowship?

When we know the encouragement, comfort, and fellowship of Christ living in us, our lives will exhibit certain characteristics. In Philippians 2:2–4, Paul contrasts these characteristics with those of people living in the power of their own flesh. **List below the distinguishing evidences of these two opposing lifestyles.**

Think about your own actions, thoughts, and reactions this last week. If you've seen any evidence of the self-life exhibited, you know there is *nothing* appealing about it. It's ugly; it stinks; in fact the self-life reeks of putrid, dead flesh—because that's what it is!

Read Romans 6:6, 11–13; Galatians 2:20; Colossians 3:3. Record what you find in each of these passages related to the following questions: Why is the self-life so rotten? Where does a self-absorbed mindset come from?

EVIDENCE OF CHRIST'S LIFE IN US	EVIDENCE OF THE SELF-LIFE IN US

The Christ life looks remarkably appealing compared to the self-life. But there is nothing *natural* about the Christ life. When we enter into a personal relationship with Jesus, we do not acquire a "Christ life button" that causes us to automatically default to a Christlike response when we are tested. Unless you live in a cave, it didn't take you long to realize that!

So how does a new Christian (or an old one, for that matter) stop living out of their dead flesh and start living the Christ life? We'll explore this question more deeply later, but for now read the following passages and record what is true of all those who are Christ followers.

• Colossians 1:27

• 2 Timothy 1:14

If Christ dwells in you through His Holy Spirit, is it possible for Christ to live His life through you? Is it possible for your life to be characterized by the Christ life rather than the self-life?

Personal Take-Aways

As you bring your time in God's Word to a close for today, prayerfully and honestly examine your own life. Are you characterized more by the Christ life or the self-life? Write out a prayer asking God to reveal the characteristics He sees in your life. Then thank Him for His grace that enables you to change.

"God is able to make all grace abound to you, so that having all sufficiency in all things at all times, you may abound in every good work" (2 Cor. 9:8 ESV).

Day Three
HUMILITY DEFINED

"Have this attitude in yourselves which was also in Christ Jesus" (Phil. 2:5). What does it mean to have the same attitude as Christ? What attitudes characterized Christ's life as He walked on this earth? How did His internal attitudes affect His external behavior? That will be the focus of our study today. Take a few minutes to pray and ask God to give you His understanding of those things that are spiritually discerned.

Read through Philippians 2:1–11. (It really is helpful if you can read it out loud.) Now answer the following questions from this passage:

- What did you learn about Christ before He became a man?

- What did Christ have to do in order to become a man?

- As a man, what position did Christ assume?

- How far did Christ go in His obedience?

- What attitude was necessary for His obedience?

- What did God do as a result of Christ's obedience?

- How will all mankind one day respond to Christ?[1]

Look up Mark 10:45. What two reasons do you see for Christ coming to earth?

For Our Zealous Friends

Read Hebrews 2:9, 14–18 and record additional insights into Christ's purpose for becoming a man.

Isn't it amazing? The incarnation. God became a man so that we might enjoy intimacy with our Creator. Oh, the wonders of God's amazing love for you and me! It reminds me of these words from the old hymn "And Can It Be?"

> He left his Father's throne above
> > (So free, so infinite his grace!);
> Emptied himself of all but love
> > And bled for Adam's helpless race.
> 'Tis mercy all, immense and free,
> > for oh, my God, it found out me!
> Amazing love! How can it be
> > That thou, my God, shouldst die for me?

May we never allow the truths of the incarnation to become mere facts or portions of a story only retold at Christmas. Let the impact of these incredible gospel truths permeate every fiber of your being. Before continuing your study, why not stop and allow yourself to once again "stand amazed in the presence of Jesus the Nazarene."

Read through Philippians 2, marking in a distinctive way every occurrence of the word *humility* or *humbled*. What did you learn?

Think of Christ laying aside His heavenly robe to put on a robe of flesh. How would you describe the attitude of Christ in coming to earth? What thoughts and feelings would He have had? Toward you? Toward His heavenly Father? Toward His own life?

Philippians 2:6–7 confuses many people. We're told that before Christ came to earth, He existed in the form of God, and that in coming to earth, He *emptied* Himself. **What does it mean that Christ emptied Himself? Did He give up a part of His divinity? Did He stop being God? Did He lay aside any of His attributes as God in order to become a man? Record your initial thoughts regarding these questions.**

WEEK 3 ■ PHILIPPIANS TWO

Understanding this truth is vital to our Christian faith. Do you have a biblical understanding of what Christ did in coming to earth? Could you explain it to someone else? Or is it still a little vague in your own mind?

Let's solidify your understanding today by considering the meaning of the Greek word translated *emptied*. Strong's Concordance gives us the following definition: "1. Emptied (#2758 – make of no reputation KJV) [used] of Christ; he laid aside equality with or the form of God."[6]

Dr. Scofield gives further insight into the concept of *emptied*. "Nothing in this passage teaches that the Eternal Word (John 1:1) emptied Himself of either His divine nature, or His attributes, *but only of the outward and visible manifestation of the Godhead*" (emphasis added).[7]

In light of what you've learned, summarize how you would explain this truth to someone else.

Personal Take-Aways

As you consider Christ's humility in coming to earth, prayerfully meditate on Psalm 22 or Isaiah 53, and write out a prayer of thanksgiving for all Christ has done in redeeming you.

"For you know the grace of our Lord Jesus Christ, that though He was rich, yet for your sake He became poor, so that you through His poverty might become rich" (2 Cor. 8:9).

Days Four and Five
HUMILITY PRACTICED

Christ humbled Himself so that we might be redeemed and so that His Father might receive glory! The Father then commands us to have the same attitude as Christ (Phil. 2:5). Almighty God not only clothed Himself in flesh and came to earth to live and die for us, but He tells us through the inspired words of Paul's letter that it is possible (and *needful*) for us to have the same attitude as Christ.

As you think of the reality of your daily life, does having the same attitude as Christ seem impossible to you? In a sense it is. Humanly speaking we will *never* work ourselves into humility of mind through good intentions, disciplined living, or even the best laid plans. In fact if you've tried, you know the frustration, discouragement, and defeat of trying to live the Christian life in the power of your own strength. But if Christ lives in you, He has the power and ability to live *through* you so that you exhibit His attitudes (not your own) toward the situations and people that come your way.

But how do we do that? What does it mean to have the mind of Christ? How do we cultivate an attitude of humility? How do we live the Christ life and not the self-life? These are the questions we want to consider as we conclude our study today on Philippians 2:1–11.

We want to stretch you a bit today in your study of God's Word by encouraging you to complete a word study. That might sound complicated, but it's really not. We know you can do it! And we'll walk you through step by step on the Internet if you're interested.

In week one you marked the key words *mind* and *attitude*. The Greek words translated *mind* and *attitude* are used a total of 11 times in Philippians. They have also been translated *to feel* (1:7), *harmony* (4:2), and *concern* (4:10).

If you have a concordance or an expository dictionary, look up the word for *mind/attitude* and write the definition below. Please don't consult a commentary yet, as you still have much "gold" to find on your own. (You may want to use the Internet steps below just for fun.)

If you don't have your own study tools, try doing a search on the Internet. (It's not hard—you may even get hooked on word studies!) One great resource is www.StudyLight.org. On the home page click "Lexicons" in the left-hand column. Then click on "Old/New Testament Greek." In the right-hand column under "Search this resource," type in the number 5426 and click "Go." (This is the Strong's number for one of the Greek words translated *mind/attitude*.) This will provide you with the definition, the various ways the word has been translated in the Scriptures, and a listing of every Scripture reference where this word is used. Don't forget to record all that you've found in the space provided on the following page.

Congratulations—if you've just completed your first word study, we knew you could do it! We are so proud of each of you for your diligence in studying and applying God's Word to your life.

Now take time to think through what you've discovered. In the space below, summarize your understanding of what it means to have the same attitude as Christ.

How does the fact that Jesus came to serve and not to be served relate to Paul's instructions in Philippians 2:3–5?

Serving and considering others as more important than ourselves requires humility. Humility requires that we see ourselves in light of what Christ did for us on the cross. John Stott said,

> Every time we look at the cross, Christ seems to be saying to us, "I am here because of you. It is your sin I am bearing, your curse I am suffering, your debt I am paying, your death I am dying." Nothing in history or in the universe cuts us down to size like the cross. All of us have inflated views of ourselves, especially in self-righteousness, until we have visited a place called Calvary. It is there, at the foot of the cross, that we shrink to our true size.[8]

Prayerfully meditate on the words of "The Cross—My Humility" on page 51. Ask God to help you personalize who _you_ are apart from the cross of Christ.

If we had not been ransomed from the bondage of sin, we would all be motivated by self-interest, self-indulgence, and a false sense of self-sufficiency, pursuing selfish ambition for the purpose of self-glorification.

"But God" (those are two of my favorite words in Scripture) redeemed us! We are forgiven, cleansed, and transformed by the life of Christ that now lives in us through His Holy Spirit.

C. J. Mahaney says it this way: "A fundamental and radical change has occurred so that you have the desire to serve others and to see God glorified. We know the inner call to lay down our lives for one another because He laid down His life for us."[9]

Laying down our lives for others is *not* natural; our flesh often screams to remain self-focused. But it *is* possible, as we choose to die to our selfish, fleshly desires and allow Christ to live through us. Paul had more to say about the "how-to's" of this process in Ephesians 4:22–32 and Colossians 3:8–17. **Read these passages and record your responsibilities as a Christ follower in the appropriate columns.**

PUT OFF	PUT ON

Personal Take-Aways

We've covered a lot of ground this week. You may want to read back through your notes just to refresh your memory. As you conclude your study, pray that God will help you personalize the truths you've seen as you reflect on these questions:

In what ways has God most recently asked you to lay down your life for others? How is He asking you to serve others, to consider others as more important than yourself? What attitudes do you need to put off and put on?

Don't leave your study today without making personal application of these truths.

The Cross—My Humility

Then Pilate had Jesus flogged with a lead-tipped whip. *He endured this beating for me.* The soldiers wove a crown of thorns and put it on his head. *He wore it for me.* And they put a purple robe on him. Then they saluted him and taunted, "Hail! King of the Jews!" *He restrained Himself for my sake.* And they struck him on the head with a reed stick, spit on him, and dropped to their knees in mock worship. *He bore their abuse and mockery for me.* When they were finally tired of mocking him, they took off the purple robe and put his own clothes on him again. Then they led him away to be crucified. *He willingly chose to follow them for me.* Carrying the cross by himself, he went to the place called Place of the Skull (in Hebrew, *Golgotha*). There they nailed him to the cross. *He hung there for me.* And Pilate posted a sign over him that read, "Jesus of Nazareth, the King of the Jews." When the soldiers had crucified Jesus, *He allowed it for me,* they divided his clothes among the four of them. They also took his robe, but it was seamless, woven in one piece from top to bottom. So they said, "Rather than tearing it apart, let's throw dice for it." This fulfilled the Scripture that says, "They divided my garments among themselves and threw dice for my clothing." So that is what they did. Two others were crucified with him, one on either side, with Jesus between them. Jesus said, "Father, forgive them, for they don't know what they are doing." *He surrendered His "right" to avenge for me.* And the soldiers gambled for his clothes by throwing dice. The crowd watched and the leaders scoffed. "He saved others," they said, "let him save himself if he is really God's Messiah, the Chosen One." *He tolerated the mocking for me.* The soldiers mocked him, too, by offering him a drink of sour wine. They called out to him, "If you are the King of the Jews, save yourself!" At noon, darkness fell across the whole land until three o'clock. Then at three o'clock Jesus called out with a loud voice, "Eloi, Eloi, lema sabachthani?" which means "My God, my God, why have you abandoned me?" *He endured unfathomable separation from His Father for me.* And suddenly, the curtain in the sanctuary of the Temple was torn down the middle. Then Jesus shouted, "Father, I entrust my spirit into your hands!" And with those words he breathed his last. *He submitted to His Father's plan for me.*

—Text taken from the New Living Translation[10]

Notes

Day One
GOD WORKS IN, WE WORK OUT

Finish this sentence (but do not use a proper name): I could be a model Christian if

it weren't for _____.

Are you surprised by how often God uses people to expose what's really in our hearts? It's not a new phenomenon; in fact, Paul addresses it this week in our study of Philippians 2:12–30.

We've already seen from Paul's writings that Christ is to be the very essence of our life. We die; Christ lives in us. If Christ lives in us, then Christ will flow out of us. And that truth is never more evident than in our relationships.

You see, the Christian life is all about relationships. It's not about gaining knowledge. It's not about what we can do for God. It's not even about what we think God wants to do through us. It's about relationships!

It begins with our relationship with Christ. He is the very core of our life *only* if we have a personal relationship with Him. Our relationship with Christ is the foundation from which our relationship with people is determined.

Think about the relationships we've seen so far in this letter to the Philippians. Paul's relationship with Christ was clearly the core of his being. That relationship exhibited itself in Paul's deep love for the Philippians. The Philippians' love for Christ had grown and matured even as their spiritual father labored and prayed for them. Christ's life was evident in the Philippians as they loved and cared for their dear friend Paul.

Do you see the cycle? Christ loves us. We respond to that love. Christ lives in us. His love flows out of us to others. Simple, right? Not exactly!

That's why Paul spends so much time, energy, and ink addressing the area of relationships in his letter—because relationships are *hard*; they take a lot of work! Let's see how that relates to "working out what God has worked in."

Are you ready to get started? Be sure you've taken time to pray—relationships done in the power of our own flesh are never pretty!

Let's begin with a bit of review so we don't forget the context of what Paul is saying. **Read Philippians 1–2 and mark on your Philippians Worksheet every reference to the word *God* (including synonyms) in a distinct way. (You may want to draw a solid yellow triangle over the word *God*.)**

After marking the text, answer the 5 Ws and an H (Who, What, When, Where, Why, How) for this word on your Key Words chart. Remember, not every marked word will answer a specific question. As you look at each marked word, ask yourself if it answers one of those questions; if it doesn't, you don't need to record it on the chart. **What did God show you about Himself in these two chapters?**

Last week, you listed every instruction Paul gave in chapter two. Record below the specific instructions found in 2:12–18. As you do, think about how each instruction relates to relationships.

Did you find the first command, to "work out your salvation with fear and trembling," a little disturbing? If salvation is a free gift—not by works but by grace through faith—then why would Paul tell the Philippians to *work out* their salvation? And since these are also God's commands to us, how are we to obey this command? And what in the world does working out our salvation have to do with relationships?

As we consider these questions, let's begin by making some simple observations from the text.[11]

- In verse 12 who is to do the work?

- In verse 13 who is doing the work?

- From verse 12 write the word that follows *work*: "Work _____ "

- From verse 13 write the two words that follow *at work*:
  "At work _____ _____ "

- Summary: We have a responsibility to _____ _____ what God
  _____ _____ us.

From your understanding of salvation, what is Paul *not* saying in these verses? List any Scriptures that support your thoughts.

The same word translated "work out" is also translated "produces" in James 1:3. Look up this passage and see what insights you gain regarding the meaning of *work out.*

Now think through all that you've just read. Knowing what Paul *didn't* mean regarding working out our salvation, what reason might he have had to include these statements in the midst of a segment addressing the Philippians' relationships with people? What do you think working out our salvation has to do with our relationships?

What is God working in us, according to verse 13?

For Our Zealous Friends

Do word studies on the words *work out*, *to will*, and *to work* from verses 12–13.
(You may want to review page 46 for help with doing an Internet word study.)

Personal Take-Aways

You have certainly had a full day of thinking! We can't wait for our discussion time when we can process all of this together. To close this day, thank God that He continually works in us until the day He calls us home. Always working, always molding and shaping us into the image of Christ.

Now take a few minutes to consider what specific things God is working in you right now. What truths is He teaching you about His character, His principles, His ways? How is that being worked out in your life? What relational opportunities is He giving you to flesh out His work in you?

Day Two
GRUMBLING AND DISPUTING

As we focus on Philippians 2:14–16 today, we promise you'll have no problem making the connection between Paul's theme of relationships and the exhortation you are about to study. (In fact, if you're like us, you may even wish the connection weren't quite so clear!)

Imagine for a moment that you live on a totally deserted island. *Alone*. (I'm imagining a Hawaiian Island, but you can be deserted wherever you like.) Got the picture in your mind? Now imagine you've been on this island for over ten years—by your own choice!

During those ten years, how much relational conflict would you have experienced? How much grumbling and disputing would have taken place? Why? Think through the obvious and explain your conclusion.

Evidently the Philippians didn't live on a deserted island, because Paul felt the need to address the issues of grumbling and disputing in his letter to them. Record what he said below and how that applies to his theme of relationships.

What's the difference between *grumbling* and *disputing*? To find out, we need to do a word study on these two words. Use whatever study resources you have to find out the definition of the original Greek words for grumbling and disputing. If you would like to try doing a word study on the Internet, you may follow the directions previously given on page 46.

The Strong's numbers you will need are 1112 and 1261.

- Grumbling (murmuring, KJV) (1112)

• Disputing (1261)

When we choose to walk in obedience to this command, Paul says we prove something to those who are unsaved. What is it that we prove?

According to 2:15, how does the unsaved world then see us?

How does this relate to our relationship with the unsaved world?

Now let's look up several cross-references in both the Old and New Testaments that will give us a broader understanding of grumbling and God's view of it. Be sure to read the context surrounding each verse. Then answer the following questions for each verse: Who grumbled, and why? What was Jesus' (or God's) response to their grumbling?

• Matthew 20:11

• Luke 15:2

• John 6:53–61

• Jude 16

• Exodus 16:2–3, 8

• Numbers 14:27-30

For Our Zealous Friends

Do word studies for *blameless, innocent,* and *children of God above reproach.*

Personal Take-Aways

Allow the Spirit of God to speak to your heart as you apply the truths of today's lesson to your own life. Don't forget to record what He is saying to you, and your response to Him.

Day Three
A LIGHT IN THE DARKNESS

Paul tells the Philippians in 2:14–15 that the way they live their lives—the attitude they exhibit—would appear as a light in a crooked and perverse generation. We want to consider this statement today as we examine what it means to be "in the world but not of the world." Let's look first at Paul's description of the world; then we'll consider our responsibility toward that world.

Reread chapter two. While the example of our life speaks to both the saved and the unsaved, which of these two groups does it seem we are "proving" ourselves to in 2:15?

Paul says our lives will be like lights in a _____ and _____ world.

Do a word study on each of these words. How do these definitions relate to the 21st-century world in which we live?

Look up the following passages and record what they say about the world and our response to it.

- 2 Corinthians 6:17

- 2 Timothy 4:10

- James 4:4b

- 1 John 2:15–17

Now contrast what you've recorded with what you find in the following Scriptures. Record God's response to the world and how that impacts our response.

- Mark 16:15

- John 3:16

Based on what you've seen, how would you describe what it means to live *in the world* but not be *of the world*?

Think of the darkest room or physical location you have ever been in. Can you almost *feel* the darkness of pitch black? Nothing is visible, therefore little is rightly understood. Moving causes you to fear, to stumble, maybe even to fall.

Now imagine that a switch is flipped and a spotlight suddenly illuminates the room. Everything changes. You can see! But for a moment you shield your eyes; the light is blinding. Then slowly, as your eyes adjust, you begin to see, to *understand* the reality of what has always existed—but you were blinded . . . by the darkness. *The light made all the difference!*

In Philippians 2:15, Paul says our lives will *appear* as lights in the world. The Greek word for appear can also be translated "shine." In your own words, describe practical ways our lives shine in the midst of a crooked and perverse world.

Personal Take-Aways

How's your light? Where has God positioned you to shine right now in the midst of a crooked and perverse world? Are you shining? Prayerfully consider these questions and record what the Spirit says to you.

Day Four
LIVING EXAMPLES

As we approach 2:19–30, it almost seems Paul's thoughts have randomly wandered off into a travel itinerary for Timothy and Epaphroditus. But have they? Or does the apostle have a purpose in bringing this section of his letter to a close with the lives of these two men?

Reread chapter two and consider all that Paul has written. Now glance back over the list of instructions found on page 35. Does it seem as if Paul's instructions, while godly and admirable, are (at least in part) practically unattainable?

You may be thinking, "If Paul knew my family, my spouse, the people I work with, the people in my neighborhood, he would understand it's just not *always* possible to flesh out the attitude or life of Christ in my relationships. Besides, who's going to look out for my interests, my welfare, if I'm *always* thinking of others?"

I don't know about you, but I'm a "give me an example" kind of learner. Don't just tell me what to do; show me how it's done. Show me those who are living it out.

I wonder if that's what Paul is doing as he verbally dictates his letter to the Philippians. I wonder if Paul didn't include these details, at least in part, so the Philippians might have living, breathing examples of all Paul had written.

In 1 Timothy 1:2, Paul describes Timothy as "my beloved son." Of all Paul's companions, none is mentioned as often or is with him as frequently as Timothy.

Read Acts 16:1–3 and record what you learn about Timothy as he first meets the great apostle.

Record any additional insights describing Timothy from the following Scriptures:

- 1 Corinthians 16:10

- 1 Timothy 5:23

- 2 Timothy 1:5–7

Epaphroditus is only mentioned here in Philippians. We will record on the chart below all that Paul says about him in his letter.

On the chart below, list what you learned about the following:

- The mind of Christ in Philippians 2:5–8

- Timothy in Philippians 2:19–24

- Epaphroditus in Philippians 2:25–30

- Paul from your study in this book

As you list the qualities of Paul, Timothy, and Epaphroditus, if possible, list them opposite the same qualities of the mind of Christ so you can note the parallels.[12]

LIVING DEMONSTRATIONS OF THE MIND OF CHRIST

Description of the Mind of Christ	Paul	Timothy	Epaphroditus

Personal Take-Aways

Allowing Christ's life to shine through us is possible! The lives of Timothy and Epaphroditus are examples of that. Does that mean they were perfect or that they never responded in their flesh? NO. It means that day after day, hundreds of times a day as they faced difficult people and situations, they were faced with a decision: respond out of the Christ life in them or respond out of the self-life.

That means there is hope for you and me to do the same—one day at a time, one choice at a time. So, how are you doing? Has your life this week more often reflected the life of Christ or the life of _____?

your name here

Write one more time the description of the mind of Christ from Philippians 2:5–8 on the following chart. Then record one or two situations (remember, situations usually involve people) where your response reflected the mind of Christ. In the last column record times when you responded out of the self-life.

Description of the mind of Christ	Your response reflected the mind of Christ	Your response reflected the self-life

Praise God for every time Christ's life shone through you, whether in the midst of a perverse and crooked world or in the midst of your own family. You are being changed into the image of Christ. Rejoice in the changes He is making in you. Ask Him to help you crucify your flesh the next time a situation arises and you're tempted to respond wrongly.

Day Five
LIVING EXAMPLES

Paul uses the phrase *day of Christ* three times in Philippians—twice in chapter one and once in chapter two. **Read through these two chapters and mark in a distinctive way the phrase *day of Christ*. Record what you learn on your Key Word chart.**

Paul also mentions the day of Christ in his letters to the Corinthians. **Look up the following verses and record what you learn. Remember to read the context of the verses.**

- 1 Corinthians 1:8

- 1 Corinthians 5:5

- 2 Corinthians 1:13–14

Do you see any correlation between the day of Christ and Paul's theme of living the Christ life within the context of relationships? Summarize what is involved in "the day of Christ."

For Our Zealous Friends

Look up the following verses and record any additional insights you gain related to the day of Christ.

- 1 Thessalonians 2:19–20

• 1 Thessalonians 3:12–13

• 1 Thessalonians 5:23

• 1 John 3:1–3

What did Paul mean when he said that he was being poured out as a drink offering on the sacrifice and service of the Philippians' faith? How does this exhibit Christ's life in Paul's thoughts, actions, and attitudes?

Personal Take-Aways

Maranatha! "Our Lord comes." How does the anticipation of the day of Christ influence your relationships? Is there a clock ticking in your heart and mind?

The Lord is coming! Perhaps *soon*—are you ready? Are you living in anticipation? On a scale of 1–10 (1 being "I thought about that once" and 10 being "I wake up in the morning and go to sleep at night realizing *this* may be the day"), how aware are you of the imminent return of our Savior? What would help you take 2 or 3 steps forward on that scale this year? What impact might that have on your family? Your friends? Your circle of influence? Your own relationship with the Lord?

Notes

Day One
CHAPTER THREE OVERVIEW

Can you believe we're already half-way through this powerful little letter? Doesn't it just seem to overflow with practical, applicable truths, not only for the Philippians but for us as well? Oh, how I pray you are not only becoming familiar with Paul and the Philippian believers, but that you are growing in intimacy with your Lord through your time in His Word. He longs for that. He created you for that purpose. He's there, even now, in the midst of your circumstances. And He is rejoicing . . . over *you*.

Before you begin your study today, take time to enjoy His presence. Revel in the wonder of His amazing love! "The LORD your God is in your midst, a victorious warrior. He will exult over you with joy, He will be quiet in His love, He will rejoice over you with shouts of joy" (Zeph. 3:17).

Your assignment today is to read Philippians 3. As you read, you will mark several **key words** to this specific chapter. Try to read the chapter at least twice. The first time, mark the words *confidence*, *flesh*, and *righteousness*. The second time, mark the words *circumcision* and *press on*.

Record on your **Key Words chart** what you discovered about each word. Remember to use words directly from the text.

Personal Take-Aways

What questions/observations/thoughts came to your mind as you read Philippians 3? What stood out to you about Christ or about being a Christ follower? Record your thoughts, and then ask God to give you a heart that longs to know Him (Phil. 3:10).

Day Two
WHAT'S CIRCUMCISION GOT TO DO WITH IT?

Paul doesn't mince words when speaking of the "false circumcision" in chapter three. You can almost hear the ice in his voice as he moves from gracious, loving, and embracing to firm, stern, and unbending. Paul is dogmatic for a reason. We'll find out why today.

Circumcision is first mentioned in Genesis 17 as God establishes His covenant with Abraham.

Read Genesis 17 and record everything you learn about circumcision.

Circumcision was clearly a sign of God's covenant with Abraham and his descendents. Was this "cutting of flesh" what saved Abraham and his descendents? Is that what brought them into a personal relationship with God?

Consider the following Scriptures as you seek to answer that question. Always remember, it's not *our* opinions or thoughts that matter. We must base our beliefs and convictions on God's Word. The point is not only *what* you believe but *why* you believe it, based on God's Word.

Read Genesis 15:6 and Romans 4:8–11, 13. Did circumcision play a role in Abraham's salvation? Explain.

In your own words, describe why you believe God established the practice of circumcision.

What did the Jews of Paul's day believe about circumcision? (Acts 15:1)

Why do you think Paul deals with the issue of circumcision in his letter to the Philippians? Remember, the Philippian church consisted primarily of Gentile believers. Why would Gentiles need to understand the truths regarding circumcision?

How does Paul contrast those who are of the false circumcision and those who are the true circumcision? How did they differ?

For Our Zealous Friends

You'll be amazed by the reasons Paul describes the Judaizers as dogs, evil workers, and false circumcision. Look in your commentaries and record all that you discover.

Personal Take-Aways

Do we in the 21ˢᵗ century struggle with understanding certain church rituals or traditions? What are some rituals or traditions people may place their confidence in today? How are they being led astray from the true meaning of the ritual?

Prayerfully ask God to show you if there are areas where you have placed confidence in a ritual or tradition. Write out your prayer below.

WHERE'S YOUR CONFIDENCE?

Confidence: *a feeling or consciousness of one's powers or of reliance on one's circumstances.* Paul says he had every right to be self-confident. He could have been listed in the Jewish "Who's Who." He was a man of great accomplishment and influence. His pedigree alone placed him among the elite of his day.

Our focus today will be on who Paul was apart from Christ. What basis did Paul have for being self-confident? In what areas might he have been tempted to place confidence in his flesh?

Speaking of flesh, don't rely on your own today. Be sure to ask God to open your eyes to understand the truths of His Word. "Then He opened their minds to understand the Scriptures" (Luke 24:45).

Let's begin by reading through chapter three. Record Paul's "résumé" from Philippians 3:5–6. Who was he? What had he accomplished?

Record what you understand Paul to mean by having "confidence in the flesh."

Do you think it's wrong to succeed or seek to accomplish great things? Explain.

Read Psalm 71:5 and Jeremiah 17:7. In the circumstances of your life in the last week, where have you placed your confidence and trust?

How do we fix our confidence on the Lord and not in our own abilities? How do we maintain our trust in Him and not in what we are able to accomplish?

Personal Take-Aways

Take time to create your own résumé. What is your pedigree? What have you accomplished? Where have you excelled? In what areas have you succeeded? What are your assets (e.g. personal, physical, educational, financial)? Where is your training? What qualities or accomplishments bring you respect, acceptance, or advancement? Where *could* your confidence be placed? Don't be bashful. Paul wasn't—he chronicled it all!

Which of these areas tempt you to place confidence in your flesh? Explain.

How do you battle these temptations? What is God using in your life today to ensure that you place no confidence in these areas?

Spend time crying out to God for help in placing no confidence in your flesh. Ask Him to show you how to crucify your flesh in the areas you have listed. Write out your prayer below. Thank Him for *whatever* tools or methods He uses to do that!

"Before they call, I will answer; and while they are still speaking, I will hear" (Isa. 65:24).

Day Four
GAINING A PROPER PERSPECTIVE

Although Paul had every reason to be self-confident, his encounter with Christ provided a new filter through which to sift life. At some point, Paul reassessed his life through this new sieve. He reevaluated where he would place his trust.

Paul's conclusions set him on a path that impacted not only his own life, the lives of the Philippian believers, and countless others, but ultimately, 2000 years later, *your* life! Amazing, isn't it?

Aren't you glad Paul had the right sieve, the right perspective? Aren't you grateful he took the time to reassess his life and correct his course?

As you begin, ask God to help you evaluate your own life today. Ask Him to give you *His* perspective on which things are gain and which are loss.

After reading Philippians 3:1–11 at least twice, record Paul's conclusions as he evaluates what was *loss* and what was *gain*.

LOSS	GAIN

At the end of Paul's reassessment of his life, what did he conclude was gain?

Do you think Paul came to this conclusion when he was converted? Why or why not?

It seems that for Paul, "knowing Christ" did not simply mean encountering Him as Savior. He seems to speak of something that was an ongoing, daily reality.

Do you think it's possible to have Christ living in you yet not "gain Christ" as Paul states in 3:8? Explain.

From Philippians 3:9–11, what evidence existed in Paul's life that he had counted all things loss in order that he might gain Christ?

What sieve do you think Paul used in concluding what was gain and what was loss?

Personal Take-Aways

What would it mean for you, personally, to count all things as rubbish in order to gain Christ and be found in His righteousness?

We know these aren't simple fill-in-the-blank answers. They require thoughtful prayer, time, and reflection. Tomorrow has been set aside for just that purpose. During the next 24 hours, ask the Holy Spirit to impress on your mind His purpose for exposing you to these truths at this point. Who knows the lives that might be impacted through what God is doing in you today!

Day Five
A TIME FOR REFLECTION

How we pray that you have been challenged this week through your study of chapter three! The goal of this time is not that we might declare, "We've studied Philippians," but that we might be *transformed* by the truths found in this letter. Oh, that our minds might be continually renewed into the likeness of Christ as we study His Word!

With that goal in mind, we want you to spend today reflecting on what you've seen, what you've learned, how the Lord has spoken to your heart, where He wants you to go from here.

Grab a cup of coffee, turn on some instrumental music, be prepared to journal your thoughts, and ***come away***. Sit at the feet of the One who longs to speak to you today. He's waiting for you.

"Come away by yourselves to a secluded place and rest a while" (Mark 6:31).

Notes

Day One
DEAD MAN LIVING (PART 1)

Think of the power God exerted to raise Christ from the dead. Imagine the desperate pull of sin and death to keep Him trapped in the grave. A crucified Christ that remained dead and buried would not have conquered sin and death. Paul said in 1 Corinthians 15:17 that if Christ had not been raised, our faith would be worthless—we would still be in our sin.

Praise God, Christ didn't remain in the grave! With resurrection power He rose from the dead and conquered sin and death. Death no longer has mastery over Him or those who belong to Him (Rom. 6:9–11). Because of that, we now have a *living hope*. We can live with great expectation because Christ lives in us. He is working in and through us with the same power that raised Christ from the dead!

These truths had a profound impact on Paul. We'll examine them today as we focus on Philippians 3:10–11. Before we begin, ask God to open the eyes of your heart to understand the wonders that are yours through the resurrection of Jesus Christ.

Begin by reading through Philippians 3 and marking in a distinct way the word *resurrection* and any phrases dealing with *knowing Christ*. Record what you learn on your **Key Words chart** for Philippians 3.

In your own words, state the goal of Paul's life from Philippians 3:10–11.

Paul wanted to know _____. He wanted to know the _____ of

Christ's _____. He wanted to know the _____ of Christ's

_____. Paul knew the only way to know Christ intimately was by

being _____ to His _____. This conformity would result in

Paul attaining the _____ from the _____.

Write out 2 Chronicles 16:9 below, then answer the following questions.

• Who is the Lord looking for continuously?

• Why is He looking for them?

The words translated *strongly support* mean "to show His might on behalf of." Think about that. God is continuously searching for someone He can display His might through! In what area do you need that might today?

Read Ephesians 1:15–23. (You may want to read several different versions.) List what is yours as a daughter of the King. What has the Father given you as a result of your spiritual birth?

In Ephesians 3:13–19, what does Paul ask the Father to give to the Ephesian believers? According to this passage, why does he ask for this?

In your own words, describe what it means that the resurrection power of Jesus Christ is at work in your life as a child of God.

Personal Take-Aways

Is there a situation or circumstance in your life that seems impossible, unchangeable, or hopeless? Maybe it's a friend or family member you've prayed about for years; maybe it's a besetting sin that has a relentless grip on your life; maybe it's a financial or relational situation that seems to only grow worse with time; or maybe it's a recent crisis that has thrown you into a tailspin emotionally, mentally, or spiritually.

What area of your life, right now, needs a touch of the same power that raised Christ from the dead? Describe the details below. Write out *why* it seems hopeless or impossible to you.

Now take a few minutes to prayerfully lay your concern before the One who raised Christ from the dead and has promised to apply the same power to your situation. Use Ephesians 1:15–19 and 3:14–21 as a basis for your prayer. Writing out your prayer can be beneficial in helping you express your thoughts.

Day Two
DEAD MAN LIVING (PART 2)

As passionate and intentional as Paul was about knowing Christ, about experiencing the power of His resurrection and the fellowship of His sufferings in daily life, he knew the path to intimacy could only be attained through death.

(Please note: We've not focused on "the fellowship of Christ's sufferings" in this passage, since we talked about the gift of suffering during week three).

Paul describes himself as a "dead man living" in Galatians 2:20. **Read this passage and then answer the following questions.**

- When does Paul say he died?

- Paul is obviously very much alive as he writes this, so what died?

- Who now lives in Paul?

- How does Paul now live?

The truths of what it means to be a "dead man (woman) living" are fundamental to the understanding of our faith. We will never walk in consistent obedience to God and His ways until we understand that when we entered into a covenant relationship with God, we died to our own plans, purposes, desires, etc. Our lives are now totally consumed with the plans, purposes, and desires of the One who redeemed us. It's no longer about us . . . it's about Christ!

Paul desperately wanted believers to grasp the truth that they were dead men through whom Christ now lived. He wove "dead man living" principles throughout his writings to the churches.

Romans 6:1–11 gives further insights into what it means that we have been crucified with Christ. Read this passage (out loud if possible) and then summarize what you find below:

- We have _____ to sin.

- Baptism (the Greek word signifies being identified or united with) symbolizes that we have been identified with Christ's _____.

- When Christ _____, we were "united with Him" in His death.

- Because our _____ was crucified, we are no longer _____ to sin.

- We don't *have* to sin—we now *choose* to sin.

- When Christ was raised from the dead, we too were raised to walk in _____ of life.

If you are in Christ, dear friend, you have died, and your life is now hidden in Christ (Col. 3:3). When people interact with you, when they see your responses, when they hear your words, when they watch you live life, it's not you they should see; it's Christ.

Paul said in Philippians 3:10 that he was *being* conformed to Christ's death. It's a process. Because of Christ's death, we have died; but we must also *choose* to die daily to our plans, ideas, desires, and wants. Paul said, "I die daily" (1 Corinthians 15:31).

We play an active part in the process of being conformed. We must choose to renew our minds so that our lives clearly reflect the image of the One who created us. We must embrace the cross in our lives as an instrument of death that will continually crucify our flesh (Luke 9:23).

When we do, we will live a supernatural life—Christ's life in us. We will attain to the resurrection from the dead. We will stay in the grave while Christ, in the power of His resurrection, lives through us. Oh, may we press on toward that goal!

Personal Take-Aways

How much of the living Christ is evident through your life? How are you responding to the process of being conformed to Christ's death? What instrument of death is God using in your life right now? Are you embracing them, or are you kicking and screaming against the instrument—maybe even against the Lord?

On page 99 you'll find a sheet entitled *Caution: "Entering In" Requires Your Death.* When we enter into a covenant relationship with God through Jesus Christ, we must die. Read through the *Caution* list and then write out your prayer asking for God's grace to help you become a "dead woman living."

PRESSING ON

In this letter to his beloved Philippian friends, Paul reminds them there is *nothing greater* than knowing Christ. Knowing Christ means we no longer strive to *earn* our righteousness; we've been *given* Christ's righteousness through faith in Him (Isa. 61:10).

Knowing Christ means we no longer labor in the power of our own strength; we have the power that raised Christ from the dead available to us.

Knowing Christ means our sufferings are not in vain; they are a gift through which we have fellowship with the One "who for the joy set before Him endured the cross" (Heb. 12:2).

Knowing Christ means we no longer live; Christ now lives in and through us.

Nothing compares to knowing Christ! It's as though Paul is cheering the Philippians on as they run this race called the Christian life.

He's rehearsed the incredible inheritance that is theirs as children of God. He's reminded them of the process of being conformed into the image of the One who humbled Himself to the point of death on a cross. He's recalled the wonder of living the resurrected life—of what it means to be a dead man living.

Then he says, "Don't forget, I'm running with you. I've not completed the race. I'm still pressing on!" You do the same. Don't give up. Stay in the game. Run to win the prize!

Today we'll consider what it means to *press on*. You've already marked the **key words** *press on*.

Record below what you discovered about Paul's pressing on. What is he pressing toward? Why? How does he press on? What's involved?

Think back through all you've seen in our study. What might it have meant, at this point in his life, for Paul to press on?

Paul pursued Christlikeness with the enthusiasm and persistence of an athlete. He took his commitment to Christ seriously! **Do a word study on the phrase** *press on*; **record what you find below.** (If you need help using www.StudyLight.org to do a word study, refer back to page 46. The Strong's number for *press on* is 1377.)

In Philippians 3:12, Paul says he presses on so that he may lay hold of that for which he was laid hold of by Christ Jesus. You'll recall that Christ dramatically laid hold of Paul on the road to Damascus (Acts 9:1–6). **Describe the reason you believe Christ laid hold of Paul. In other words, what is it that Paul is pressing on to lay hold of?**

In our first week of study, you reflected on the time when God first opened your eyes to see your need of a Savior. **Why do you think Almighty God, the Creator of the universe, the sovereign King, would stoop down and lay hold of you? Record your initial thoughts and then read the following Scriptures for further insights: Psalm 16:3; 149:4; Isaiah 62:5; Zephaniah 3:17.**

Paul says in 3:14, "I press on toward the goal for the prize." This one who had once been zealous in persecuting the church is now zealous in his pursuit of knowing and serving Christ. He's laboring, intentionally pursuing, striving for the goal, the prize.

What is Paul's two-point strategy for reaching the goal (v. 13)?

List some of what Paul chose to forget. What things lay in his past?

Paul says he chose to focus on what lay ahead. What might some of those things have been?

It seems Paul has set some specific goals for his life. What happens if we don't have identifiable goals in our spiritual lives?

For Our Zealous Friends

The Scriptures are filled with exhortations related to living life intentionally. Read the following Scriptures and note ways we're instructed to live: Mark 13:23, 33; Luke 21:34–36; 1 Thessalonians 5:1–11; 1 Peter 1:13; 1 John 3:2–3.

Personal Take-Aways

How intentional are you in your relationship with Christ? Are you pressing on to know Him, or are you hoping that knowing Him just happens?

Record below ways in which you are purposefully pressing on toward the goal of knowing Christ more intimately.

If you've never thought through specific goals related to growing in your relationship with Christ, take the time to do that right now. Record any specific goals and what it will take to reach them. Do you need accountability? Who will that be?

Tell God of your desire to know Him more intimately. I can't think of anything He longs to hear more.

Day Four
ENEMIES OF THE CROSS

Begin your day by reading Philippians 3.

In the midst of a letter of gratitude overflowing with the theme of rejoicing, we suddenly find Paul weeping. Read 3:17–19 and record the cause of Paul's tears.

List the description Paul gives of those who are enemies of the cross.

Think about what the cross means in a Christian's life. Read the following passages and record your insights before answering the question.

• Matthew 10:34–39

• Luke 14:25–35

• Galatians 2:19–21

WEEK 6 ■ PHILIPPIANS THREE

Why do you think Paul calls these people enemies of the cross?

Do you think those mentioned in 3:2 are related to these enemies of the cross mentioned in verse 18? If so, how? Why?

Personal Take-Aways

Are there those today who would be considered enemies of the cross? How would you identify them?

Are enemies of the cross only found outside the church walls? Explain.

How can you guard against following after wrong examples?

CITIZENS OF HEAVEN

Think back to the last time you *eagerly* awaited something or someone. Maybe it was a dream vacation, your wedding day, the birth of a child, a reunion with family or friends, or even the purchase of your own home.

Whatever the event, do you recall how it consumed your thoughts? How you meticulously planned the rest of your life around that special time? How you thought, talked, and dreamed of all that would take place? As the time drew near, your focus became increasingly single-minded . . . until *finally* the moment arrived!

We'll see that same eager anticipation filling Paul's heart as he pens this last segment of chapter three. **One last time, read Philippians 3:17–21.**

What was Paul eagerly awaiting?

Eternally speaking, where is your citizenship?

If you are a citizen of heaven, what terms could be used to describe your stay here on earth? Read the following Scriptures for additional help identifying your time on earth: Hebrews 11:13–16; 1 Peter 1:2; 2:11.

If you've traveled in a foreign country, you may remember what it means to feel different, to stand out in a crowd, or to be misunderstood. **Have you, as a citizen of heaven, ever experienced those same feelings while living here on earth? Explain.**

In Philippians 3:19–20, Paul contrasts those who set their mind on earthly things with those who set their mind on heavenly (eternal) things. **Read Colossians 3:1–3 and describe what helps you set your mind on things above.**

Personal Take-Aways

As you conclude your time in the Word today, how would you characterize the things that consume your mind? Are you generally more focused on earthly, temporal things that 100 years from now will not matter? Or is your heart more often focused on the eternal, things that will endure, things that matter to the heart of God?

Reflect on these questions and record your thoughts below.

Caution

"Entering In" Requires Your Death.

Death to:

your independence,

your plans,

your desires,

your way of thinking,

your way of feeling,

your way of acting,

your passions,

your personal rights,

your time,

your energy,

your money,

your reputation,

your friends . . .

"Entering In" will cost you your life.

Notes

Day One
CHAPTER FOUR OVERVIEW

As Paul draws this letter to a close, he holds nothing back in reaffirming the depth of his love for the Philippian believers. Having warned, exhorted, and refocused the hearts and minds of his beloved friends, Paul still has much to say before ending this letter. You'll be amazed by all he squeezes into the remaining 23 verses.

Read chapter four at least twice. Record every instruction Paul gives, along with the reference, on the Instructions in Philippians chart located in the appendix.

Personal Take-Aways

You have been incredibly faithful in applying yourself to the study of Philippians. We are so proud of your diligence in pursuing truth and desiring to know the One who is Truth!

That's really the essence of Bible study: that we might become more intimately acquainted with who God is—His character, His attributes, His ways—and that our lives might be transformed by the truth of His Word. How we pray that you have encountered the living God intimately and are experiencing the wonder of living in the light of His truths as a result of the time you've spent in Philippians.

Please reread your list of instructions from chapter four. Quiet your heart and allow the Spirit of God to speak to you. Which of these instructions does He want to apply to your life today—to the circumstances, people, and situations in the midst of your reality? Ask Him! He promises to tell you. Record the thoughts He impresses on your mind, and your response to Him.

THE DREADED "C" WORD

Conflict! What's your initial response to a "glitch" that causes relational conflict at some level? How do you respond when you realize the "C" word has crept into one of your relationships?

Whether its marital conflict, conflict with children, or relational conflict in the church or workplace, few of us *enjoy* conflict. Yet conflict is a very real part of life—even the Christian life. The Philippian church was no exception.

Paul spent considerable time reminding the Philippians that their relationship with Christ—the fact that Christ now lived *in* them—would have a direct impact on their relationship with others. They could not glory in the wonder of all they possessed in Christ and all that awaited them in heaven while living self-absorbed, selfish, conceited lives. Six times, Paul encouraged the believers to abandon their selfishness and serve others.

In chapter four, Paul's generalizations become pointedly personal. There was "trouble in the camp" at Philippi, and Paul was not about to deny it or pretend it didn't exist. There was far too much at stake!

Read Philippians 4:1–7. Remember, this is a handwritten letter that would have been read aloud to all those in the church at Philippi.

What do you learn from this passage about Euodia and Syntyche?

What instruction does Paul give to these two women? Does Paul tell us who is at fault in this conflict? Why do you think he handled the conflict in this way?

Were other people to play any role in bringing resolution to this conflict? Explain.

Read the following Scriptures and note any further insights you glean regarding handling conflict within the body of Christ. Who is responsible to seek peace? Why is it important to resolve conflict? What happens if conflict is not resolved?

• Matthew 5:23–24

• Matthew 18:15–20

• John 13:35

• Romans 12:18

• Colossians 3:12–15

• 1 Peter 1:22–23

Conflict is a normal part of life; it happens! It was obviously happening in the church at Philippi. Yet Paul saw no need to discuss the root of the conflict, only the importance of resolving it.

Unresolved conflict has the potential to be far more destructive than whatever pre-cipitated the conflict in the beginning. **Describe below any negative consequences you have personally seen from conflict that was, in some way, mishandled.**

What positive results have you seen from handling a conflict biblically?

Personal Take-Aways

"Whatever happens, conduct yourselves in a manner worthy of the gospel of Christ" (Phil. 1:27 NIV). Since conflict is a real part of the Christian life, we will deal with it, one way or another. How do you handle conflict? Ken Sande, author of *The Peacemaker*, says we are either peace-fakers, peace-breakers, or peace-makers.

Can you imagine if the only thing recorded about your life was that you were *not* known as a peacemaker? We know nothing else about Euodia and Syntyche except that the conflict in their relationship was negatively affecting the peace of the Philippian church. News of their struggle had journeyed some 800 miles to Paul in Rome!

Paul's "true comrade" was evidently known to be a peacemaker. Paul feels confident that he will pay the price to help Euodia and Syntyche bring resolution to the issues that are dividing them.

What about you? Are you characterized by being a peace-faker, a peace-breaker, or a peace-maker? What if the one sentence recorded about your life reflected how you handled conflict—what would it say?

Is there an area of relational conflict in your life right now? How are you handling it? What steps have you taken to resolve the conflict?

What steps do you need to take in ordered to be reconciled with this individual?

Take time to commit this situation to the Lord in prayer. Verbalize to Him your commitment to live at peace with all men, as far as it depends on you (Rom. 12:18).

Days Three and Four
REJOICE OR WORRY

Do you find it interesting that, on the heels of addressing conflict among the brethren, the very next words that flow from Paul's pen are, "Rejoice in the Lord always"?

I don't know about you, but my first thought in the middle of conflict of any kind is not typically "rejoice." Maybe that's why Paul repeated the exhortation, so we wouldn't miss this point: *Joy in the midst* of whatever we are facing is possible!

I can almost see Paul as he sits, under house arrest, penning these words to his beloved friends. *Rejoice in the Lord always.* He's a man awaiting trial—a trial that could potentially lead to his death—a trial he's been awaiting for several years! The waiting has been wracked with adversity, pain, heartache, and relentless difficulty.

Yet as Paul writes, he seems to be saying, "However difficult things are, whatever conflict you are facing, whatever hardship or trial awaits you, whatever situation is stretching you far beyond what you ever imagined possible . . . **in the midst of that trial** . . . *choose joy!*"

Paul isn't writing beyond where he's living. His life loudly proclaims the reality of rejoicing in the Lord always. The Philippians have been exhorted to follow his example. As have we. We'll examine how to do that as we continue our study in Philippians 4.

To put us in the context of all Paul is saying, read Philippians 3:12–4:7. (Remember, this is a personal letter; originally, there were no chapter and verse divisions.)

Philippians 4:4–6 contrasts the two choices we each face daily. Will we rejoice or will we be _____?

The Greek word translated *rejoice* means "be glad, be delighted, rejoice exceedingly." Humanly speaking it seems counter-intuitive to think that we can be "exceedingly delighted" in the midst of trials and hardship.

Read the following Scriptures and record any insights you find, including the reason given for rejoicing, and how we can implement the practice of *joy in the midst* in our daily lives.

• Psalm 31:7

• Psalm 90:14

• Romans 12:12

In a concordance, expository dictionary, or any other study tool you might have, look up the words *anxious* and *nothing* in verse 6 and the word *gentle* in verse 5. Record what you find. (If you don't have access to these resources, we've included a "cheat sheet" for you at the end of this lesson.)

Do you think it's possible to rejoice and be anxious at the same time? Explain.

Paul gives a sure cure for worry in verses 4–7 of this chapter. Record his instructions on the following chart. Be sure to include the references. Then write an explanation of each instruction so that someone else could implement the sure cure for a worry-free life.[13]

HOW TO STOP WORRYING

INSTRUCTION	EXPLANATION

In one sentence describe the antidote to worry.

What is promised if we will apply this antidote?

Personal Take-Aways

Someone may ask, "Can a Christian be filled with worry and fear?" The answer: Absolutely! *But why would we?* Let's personalize that as we conclude our time today.

What causes *you* to worry or fear? What has to happen (or not happen) before anxiety creeps into your heart and mind?

How are you doing at applying the truths of Philippians 4:4–7? When was the last opportunity you had to rejoice *always*? To allow others to see your gentle, gracious spirit *in the midst*? What were you in the midst of the last time the Lord whispered, *"I am near!"*?

On a scale of 1–10, how would you rate the intimacy level of your prayer life in the last month?

Are you characterized more by rejoicing or anxiety? How is this connected to your prayer life?

What steps do you need to take to become obedient to the Lord's exhortation to *rejoice in the Lord **always**?* Will you? Write out a prayer expressing your need and your commitment. If it will help, ask a friend to hold you accountable to choose joy in the midst of your daily circumstances.

Cheat Sheet

- Gentle spirit (#1933 – *moderation* KJV)—seemingly suitable, equitable, fair, mild, gentle, considerate

- Anxious (#3309)—to be troubled with cares, to seek to promote your interests; from #4305, to be anxious ahead of time, to take thought of, to worry

- Nothing (#3367)—not even one thing!

Day Five
THINK ON THESE THINGS (PART 1)

Are you a "check it off the list" person? I *love* lists! They help me organize, prioritize, and visualize all I need to do. *And* they create a built-in reward system. There's just nothing like laying your head on the pillow, knowing that your list for the day has been completed (or at least transferred to tomorrow's list).

In Philippians 4:8, Paul gives list makers great reason to rejoice. He provides a list that will help us choose joy. He says, "Think on these things."

We're going to examine Paul's list closely next week. But for today, we thought it would be wise to give you time to think on different things—those things you have already studied this week.

So often we rush from one lesson, one teaching, one truth to the next. We miss the joy of simply sitting at the feet of the One who says, "Be still and **know** that I am God"— in the midst of conflict, in the midst of those situations that are causing you great anxiety right now—in the midst of life!

So for today, simply sit and reflect on what God has been showing you this week. Spend time talking with the Lord. Then just listen for the voice of His Holy Spirit. "Before they call, I will answer; and while they are still speaking, I will hear" (Isa. 65:24).

You may want to begin by focusing on the wonder of the One who desires to speak to you. The quote on the following page comes from *31 Days of Praise* by Ruth Myers. Scripture references are listed at the end. You may use this space to record your thoughts, God's words, and your prayers.

My heart rejoices in You, Lord,

for You are my *strong shelter* in times of trouble

and danger and stress, my *hiding place*

to whom I may *continually resort* . . . my Father

who lovingly provides for me . . . *my Shepherd*

who *guides and protects* me . . . my Champion

who upholds my cause as *His child*

and *defends* my highest interests . . .

my Bridegroom who *delights* in me . . .

my God who is *mighty to save,*

who *rests in His love* for me

and *rejoices* over me with singing, with shouts of joy.

You are my *inheritance*, my share in life,

the One who *satisfies* my longing soul

and fills my hungry soul with *goodness.*

I praise You for Your *love* and Your wisdom.

You are too *wise* to ever make a mistake,

too *loving* to ever do anything unkind.

You act on my behalf,

accomplishing what concerns me

and *fulfilling Your purpose* for me as I call on You. . . .

How *precious is Your love* to me, O God!

I sing for *joy* as I take *refuge* in the shadow of Your wings!

(Psalm 27:5; 71:3; 91:1–2; Matthew 6:25–26; Psalm 23:1–3; Isaiah 62:5; Zephaniah 3:17–18; Psalm 16:5–6; 107:9; Psalm 57:2; 138:8; Psalm 36:7; Psalm 63:7)[14]

Notes

Days One and Two
THINK ON THESE THINGS (PART 2)

Congratulations! You've made it to the final week in our study of Philippians. Just think of all you've seen and learned as we've journeyed through these four short chapters of Paul's letter. Have you felt at times like you were drinking from a fire hydrant? Gulping to take in all that flowed from Paul's heart?

Can you imagine the Philippians trying to take it all in as they listened to the reading of Paul's words? Surely they must have come again and again, perhaps one at a time, to sit and reread the words so carefully penned by their spiritual father. To drink in the fullness of all he had communicated; the indescribable joy, the unavoidable conviction, the affirmations, the challenges. . . . Wouldn't you love to have overheard their discussions as they sought to implement and apply all they had heard?

There was much to be done! Conflicts needed resolving, attitudes needed adjusting, priorities needed refocusing, worries needed to be left behind, false teachers needed to be addressed, suffering needed to be reevaluated, and a passionate love relationship with Jesus needed to be intentionally pursued.

I wonder if their minds were a bit overwhelmed. Perhaps Paul anticipated that, as his thoughts and words turn again to the subject of the mind. He has visited this topic frequently in his letter; 11 times in all he speaks of our mind or attitude. Paul knew that one of our biggest battles would be waged in the mind. In light of that, he gives a command that will revolutionize our thinking *if we will heed it.*

We want to examine Paul's revolutionary command today, but before we head out to the battlefield, be sure you've taken time to pray; an unprepared, ill-equipped soldier is a danger to himself and others! "If you follow these instructions, you will fight like a good soldier" (1 Tim. 1:18 CEV).

Read Philippians 4:1–9 in two different versions.

Paul gives specific instructions in Philippians 4:8 that are followed by an incredible promise. It seems the promise rests on the fulfillment of certain conditions or instructions. On the next page, record the promise from v. 9 and the conditions for the promise to be fulfilled from vv. 8–9.

• Promise:

• Conditions:

Paul says, "Practice these things, and you will experience God's peace." Do them continually, repeatedly, habitually. Don't ever think you can take the day off or that you've matured beyond the point of needing to think on these things.

How have you seen evidence in Paul's life that *he* was choosing to think on these things; that he was running his thoughts through this grid of truth? Recall all you know about Paul's circumstances, and then record how his life exemplified these truths.

Do a word study on the word *dwell* in 4:8, and record what you find.
(The Strong's number is 3049.)

In Philippians 4:6–7, Paul dealt with worry, prayer, and the peace of God. How do you think verse 8 relates to verses 6–7?

Read Isaiah 26:3. How does it relate to Philippians 4:6–9?

Describe a time when you experienced God's peace as a result of fixing your mind on Him and all that is true because of Him.

Describe a time when you lacked God's peace because you were not fixing your mind on the Lord.

How is our trust in God related to what we dwell on?

In 2 Corinthians 10:3–5, Paul gives further battle instructions related to our minds. Read this passage and then answer the following questions:

• Describe the weapons of warfare mentioned in these verses. What are they? What are they not?

• Based on what you've already studied regarding God's power, what do you know about the power of these weapons?

• What do these weapons destroy?

• What are the weapons Paul is speaking of? What destroys the things you have listed above? (Eph. 6:10–18 gives additional insights.)

• The specific battles Paul describes take place in the mind. What does he say we are doing with our mind? Describe in your own words what this means.

Personal Take-Aways

Well, how was the battle for *your* mind this last week? Have you seen victory? Minor defeats? Catastrophic loss? What thoughts are running across your radar screen? Are there unwanted thoughts assaulting you on a regular basis?

Take time to describe the battles that are being waged in your mind.

How do these compare with the thought grid found in Philippians 4:8?

What would it look like for you to take the thoughts that are plaguing your mind and bring them captive to the truth? What practical steps could you take in doing that? What would it require of you? Are you willing to engage in this warfare of taking your thoughts captive, or are you content to be held captive in your mind?

If you are ready to engage, write out your prayer of commitment to the Lord below. Then verbalize your commitment to one person. No soldier would ever consider entering a battlefield alone, without those he depended on for support. Accountability is essential in fighting this battle for your mind!

Days Three and Four

THE JOY OF CONTENTMENT

If the mind is a battlefield, then contentment is one of the greatest battles being fought there. Oh, how we struggle to be satisfied! If we aren't struggling with our body shape, it's the size or location or décor of our house. Or our car. Or our sound system, computer system, or even our cell phone.

And if possessions aren't your struggle, then what about your marriage relationship? Are you content with the husband God gave you? What about your children? Your job?

It seems we are constantly assaulted with a barrage of things that tempt us to become discontent. *Big* money is spent and countless brain cells expended to develop more innovative ways to breed discontentment. It's called advertising!

Yet it seems that the battle for contentment is not only a modern-day problem. Paul addresses the issue with his Philippian friends and admits that he himself—one of the most highly educated and intellectual men of his day—had to *learn* to be content.

If contentment is learned, then it must not come naturally. So how do we learn it? Is there a formula? A course we can take? A book we can read? Better yet, isn't there a pill that will instantly transform our discontented minds?

This will be the focus of our attention for these last days in Philippians. But please do not be content to complete today's study without crying out for the Lord's wisdom, direction, and help in applying the truths of His Word to your life.

Read Philippians 4:4–17. Keep in mind all Paul has experienced and the current conditions in which he is living (see 2 Corinthians 4:8–12).

Describe the specific areas Paul mentions in which he has learned to be content.

If contentment isn't natural, what *does* come naturally? How is this exhibited in our lives?

What does Paul say is the secret to this contentment?

How does knowing the source of our strength breed contentment?

Paul may have experienced "humble means" during the time the Philippians lacked opportunity to provide for him. Do you sense any bitterness or discontentment as a result? Why do you think that is?

In Philippians 4:15, Paul hints at further issues that could have bred bitterness. How do you think he avoided a root of bitterness from taking hold in his heart? What grid must he have been thinking through? What truths must he have dwelt on?

Read the following Scriptures and note how they relate to contentment in our everyday life.

- 1 Chronicles 29:11–13

- Romans 8:28–29

How do Philippians 4:10–13 and Philippians 2:14 relate to each other?

How would the principle of taking our thoughts captive (2 Cor. 10:3–5) relate to our battle for contentment?

Throughout his letter to the Philippians, Paul, inspired by the Holy Spirit, has masterfully woven truths concerning Jesus, rejoicing, and the mind (attitude). In his closing thoughts, Paul's contentment *whatever the circumstances* becomes even more evident.

Describe below how you perceive contentment being related to Jesus, rejoicing, and the mind (attitude).

Personal Take-Aways

The battlefields of our minds are littered with land mines set to explode in discontentment at any moment. It's vital, then, that we diligently study the lay of the land so we can avoid the land mines and learn ways to clear our minds of that which can so quickly destroy our joy and contentment.

In what areas do you struggle with discontentment in your life? Relationally? Physically? Materially?

What are the internal or external indicators that occur as a result of your discontentment? In other words, what do you think, say, or do that reveals a level of discontentment in your heart?

What are the triggers that cause you to stumble in the areas you have mentioned? It might be mail order catalogs, shopping malls, certain types of movies/ books/music, certain topics of discussion, etc.

What practical steps can you take to avoid the ignition of discontentment in your life?

Contentment is an attitude, a mindset that must be learned. It needs to be developed within a framework of Scripture. You would be wise to develop an arsenal of biblical truths you can dwell on whenever you are tempted to become discontented or when you know you are entering a zone filled with land mines (like the mall!).

Use this space to begin assembling your arsenal. Then begin to load the ammunition in your mind and heart through memorization. We've given you a few pieces of artillery to help you get started!

- Set your mind on the things above, not on the things that are on earth (Col. 3:2).

- For the sake of Christ, then, I am content with weaknesses, insults, hardships, persecutions, and calamities. For when I am weak, then I am strong (2 Cor. 12:10 ESV).

- But if we have food and clothing, we will be content with that (1 Tim. 6:8 NIV).

A LOOK BACK

Well, dear friend, you have finished the course. You have faithfully run the race of applying yourself to the study and application of God's Word. *We are so proud of you.* How we pray that your life will be forever impacted by the truths you have discovered in Paul's letter to the Philippians! May you daily press on toward the goal of knowing Christ more intimately. Oh, what a celebration we will have at the finish line!

As you conclude this study, it would be beneficial for you to reflect on the most significant things God has shown you during your time in Philippians. What are your top 3 take-aways?

Spend time today looking back through your notes and recording your thoughts. These questions may help you get started: What has God impressed on your heart during this study? How have you been encouraged, convicted, or challenged? What areas of obedience has God challenged you in? How has your life been touched by Paul's? By the Philippians'? How has your thinking been impacted?

May the evidence of Christ's life in you become increasingly magnified as you persevere in dying to your flesh and living in the incredible power that raised Christ from the dead.

Maranatha!

Notes

Notes

BOOK OF PHILIPPIANS

CHAPTER 1

1 Paul and Timothy, bond-servants of Christ Jesus, to all the saints in

Christ Jesus who are in Philippi, including the overseers and deacons:

2 Grace to you and peace from God our Father and the Lord Jesus Christ.

3 I thank my God in all my remembrance of you,

4 always offering prayer with joy in my every prayer for you all,

5 in view of your participation in the gospel from the first day until now.

6 For I am confident of this very thing, that He who began a good

work in you will perfect it until the day of Christ Jesus.

7 For it is only right for me to feel this way about you all, because

I have you in my heart, since both in my imprisonment and in the

defense and confirmation of the gospel, you all are partakers of

grace with me.

8 For God is my witness, how I long for you all with the affection

of Christ Jesus.

9 And this I pray, that your love may abound still more and more in

real knowledge and all discernment,

10 so that you may approve the things that are excellent, in order to be

sincere and blameless until the day of Christ;

11 having been filled with the fruit of righteousness which comes

through Jesus Christ, to the glory and praise of God.

12 Now I want you to know, brethren, that my circumstances have

turned out for the greater progress of the gospel,

13 so that my imprisonment in the cause of Christ has become well

known throughout the whole praetorian guard and to everyone else,

14 and that most of the brethren, trusting in the Lord because of my

imprisonment, have far more courage to speak the word of God

without fear.

15 Some, to be sure, are preaching Christ even from envy and strife,

but some also from good will;

16 the latter do it out of love, knowing that I am appointed for the

defense of the gospel;

17 the former proclaim Christ out of selfish ambition rather than from

pure motives, thinking to cause me distress in my imprisonment.

18 What then? Only that in every way, whether in pretense or in truth,

Christ is proclaimed; and in this I rejoice. Yes, and I will rejoice,

19 for I know that this will turn out for my deliverance through your

prayers and the provision of the Spirit of Jesus Christ,

20 according to my earnest expectation and hope, that I will not be put

to shame in anything, but that with all boldness, Christ will even

now, as always, be exalted in my body, whether by life or by death.

21 For to me, to live is Christ and to die is gain.

22 But if I am to live on in the flesh, this will mean fruitful labor for

me; and I do not know which to choose.

23 But I am hard-pressed from both directions, having the desire to

depart and be with Christ, for that is very much better;

24 yet to remain on in the flesh is more necessary for your sake.

25 Convinced of this, I know that I will remain and continue with you

all for your progress and joy in the faith,

26 so that your proud confidence in me may abound in Christ Jesus

through my coming to you again.

27 Only conduct yourselves in a manner worthy of the gospel of

Christ, so that whether I come and see you or remain absent, I will

hear of you that you are standing firm in one spirit, with one mind

striving together for the faith of the gospel;

28 in no way alarmed by your opponents—which is a sign of destruction

for them, but of salvation for you, and that too, from God.

29 For to you it has been granted for Christ's sake, not only to believe

in Him, but also to suffer for His sake,

30 experiencing the same conflict which you saw in me, and now hear

to be in me.

CHAPTER 2

1 Therefore if there is any encouragement in Christ, if there is any

consolation of love, if there is any fellowship of the Spirit, if any

affection and compassion,

2 make my joy complete by being of the same mind, maintaining the

same love, united in spirit, intent on one purpose.

3 Do nothing from selfishness or empty conceit, but with humility of

mind regard one another as more important than yourselves;

4 do not merely look out for your own personal interests, but also for

the interests of others.

5 Have this attitude in yourselves which was also in Christ Jesus,

6 who, although He existed in the form of God, did not regard equality

with God a thing to be grasped,

7 but emptied Himself, taking the form of a bond-servant, and being

made in the likeness of men.

8 Being found in appearance as a man, He humbled Himself by

becoming obedient to the point of death, even death on a cross.

9 For this reason also, God highly exalted Him, and bestowed on Him

the name which is above every name,

10 so that at the name of Jesus EVERY KNEE WILL BOW, of those who are

in heaven and on earth and under the earth,

11 and that every tongue will confess that Jesus Christ is Lord, to the

glory of God the Father.

12 So then, my beloved, just as you have always obeyed, not as in my

presence only, but now much more in my absence, work out your

salvation with fear and trembling;

13 for it is God who is at work in you, both to will and to work for

His good pleasure.

14 Do all things without grumbling or disputing;

15 so that you will prove yourselves to be blameless and innocent,

children of God above reproach in the midst of a crooked and

perverse generation, among whom you appear as lights in the world,

16 holding fast the word of life, so that in the day of Christ I will have

reason to glory because I did not run in vain nor toil in vain.

17 But even if I am being poured out as a drink offering upon the sacrifice

and service of your faith, I rejoice and share my joy with you all.

18 And you too, I urge you, rejoice in the same way and share your joy

with me.

19 But I hope in the Lord Jesus to send Timothy to you shortly, so that

I also may be encouraged when I learn of your condition.

20 For I have no one else of kindred spirit who will genuinely be

concerned for your welfare.

21 For they all seek after their own interests, not those of Christ Jesus.

22 But you know of his proven worth, that he served with me in the

furtherance of the gospel like a child serving his father.

23 Therefore I hope to send him immediately, as soon as I see how

things go with me;

24 and I trust in the Lord that I myself also will be coming shortly.

25 But I thought it necessary to send to you Epaphroditus, my brother

and fellow worker and fellow soldier, who is also your messenger

and minister to my need;

26 because he was longing for you all and was distressed because you

had heard that he was sick.

27 For indeed he was sick to the point of death, but God had mercy on

him, and not on him only but also on me, so that I would not have

sorrow upon sorrow.

28 Therefore I have sent him all the more eagerly so that when you see

him again you may rejoice and I may be less concerned about you.

29 Receive him then in the Lord with all joy, and hold men like him in

high regard;

30 because he came close to death for the work of Christ, risking his

life to complete what was deficient in your service to me.

CHAPTER 3

1 Finally, my brethren, rejoice in the Lord. To write the same things

again is no trouble to me, and it is a safeguard for you.

2 Beware of the dogs, beware of the evil workers, beware of the false

circumcision;

3 for we are the true circumcision, who worship in the Spirit of God

and glory in Christ Jesus and put no confidence in the flesh,

4 although I myself might have confidence even in the flesh. If anyone

else has a mind to put confidence in the flesh, I far more:

5 circumcised the eighth day, of the nation of Israel, of the tribe of

Benjamin, a Hebrew of Hebrews; as to the Law, a Pharisee;

6 as to zeal, a persecutor of the church; as to the righteousness which is

in the Law, found blameless.

7 But whatever things were gain to me, those things I have counted as

loss for the sake of Christ.

8 More than that, I count all things to be loss in view of the surpassing

value of knowing Christ Jesus my Lord, for whom I have suffered the loss

of all things, and count them but rubbish so that I may gain Christ,

9 and may be found in Him, not having a righteousness of my own

derived from the Law, but that which is through faith in Christ, the

righteousness which comes from God on the basis of faith,

10 that I may know Him and the power of His resurrection and the

fellowship of His sufferings, being conformed to His death;

11 in order that I may attain to the resurrection from the dead.

12 Not that I have already obtained it or have already become perfect,

but I press on so that I may lay hold of that for which also I was laid

hold of by Christ Jesus.

13 Brethren, I do not regard myself as having laid hold of it yet; but

one thing I do: forgetting what lies behind and reaching forward to

what lies ahead,

14 I press on toward the goal for the prize of the upward call of God in

Christ Jesus.

15 Let us therefore, as many as are perfect, have this attitude; and if in

anything you have a different attitude, God will reveal that also to you;

16 however, let us keep living by that same standard to which we have

attained.

17 Brethren, join in following my example, and observe those who

walk according to the pattern you have in us.

18 For many walk, of whom I often told you, and now tell you even

weeping, that they are enemies of the cross of Christ,

19 whose end is destruction, whose god is their appetite, and whose

glory is in their shame, who set their minds on earthly things.

20 For our citizenship is in heaven, from which also we eagerly wait for

a Savior, the Lord Jesus Christ;

21 who will transform the body of our humble state into conformity

with the body of His glory, by the exertion of the power that He has

even to subject all things to Himself.

CHAPTER 4

1 Therefore, my beloved brethren whom I long to see, my joy and

crown, in this way stand firm in the Lord, my beloved.

2 I urge Euodia and I urge Syntyche to live in harmony in the Lord.

3 Indeed, true companion, I ask you also to help these women who

have shared my struggle in the cause of the gospel, together with

Clement also and the rest of my fellow workers, whose names are in

the book of life.

4 Rejoice in the Lord always; again I will say, rejoice!

5 Let your gentle spirit be known to all men. The Lord is near.

6 Be anxious for nothing, but in everything by prayer and supplication

with thanksgiving let your requests be made known to God.

7 And the peace of God, which surpasses all comprehension, will guard

your hearts and your minds in Christ Jesus.

8 Finally, brethren, whatever is true, whatever is honorable, whatever is

right, whatever is pure, whatever is lovely, whatever is of good repute,

if there is any excellence and if anything worthy of praise, dwell on

these things.

9 The things you have learned and received and heard and seen in me,

practice these things, and the God of peace will be with you.

10 But I rejoiced in the Lord greatly, that now at last you have revived

your concern for me; indeed, you were concerned before, but you

lacked opportunity.

11 Not that I speak from want, for I have learned to be content in

whatever circumstances I am.

12 I know how to get along with humble means, and I also know how

to live in prosperity; in any and every circumstance I have learned the

secret of being filled and going hungry, both of having abundance

and suffering need.

13 I can do all things through Him who strengthens me.

14 Nevertheless, you have done well to share with me in my affliction.

15 You yourselves also know, Philippians, that at the first preaching of

the gospel, after I left Macedonia, no church shared with me in the

matter of giving and receiving but you alone;

16 for even in Thessalonica you sent a gift more than once for my needs.

17 Not that I seek the gift itself, but I seek for the profit which increases

to your account.

18 But I have received everything in full and have an abundance; I am

amply supplied, having received from Epaphroditus what you have

sent, a fragrant aroma, an acceptable sacrifice, well-pleasing to God.

19 And my God will supply all your needs according to His riches in

glory in Christ Jesus.

20 Now to our God and Father be the glory forever and ever. Amen.

21 Greet every saint in Christ Jesus. The brethren who are with me

greet you.

22 All the saints greet you, especially those of Caesar's household.

23 The grace of the Lord Jesus Christ be with your spirit.

People in Philippians

People in Philippians

People in Philippians

People in Philippians

Key Words

Key Words

Key Words

Key Words

Key Words

Endnotes

1. Jerry Bridges, *The Discipline of Grace* (Colorado Springs, Col.: NavPress, 1994), 46.

2. *Precept Upon Precept Philippians* (Chattanooga, TN: Precept Ministries International, 2000), 32.

3. Ibid., 45.

4. Ibid.

5. *The Adam Clarke Commentary* is a derivative of an electronic edition prepared by GodRules.net.

6. *Strong's Concordance*: http://www.studylight.org/isb/view.cgi?number=2758

7. *Scofield Reference Notes* (1917 Edition): http://www.studylight.org/com/srn/view.cgi?book=php&chapter=002

8. John Stott, *The Cross of Christ* (Downers Grove, Ill; InterVarsity Press,1968), 12.

9. C. J. Mahaney, *Humility, True Greatness* (Sisters, Oregon; Multnomah Publishers, Inc., 2005), 58.

10. Scripture compiled from Matthew 27, Mark 15–16, Luke 23, and John 18–19.

11. *Precept Upon Precept Philippians*, 68.

12. Ibid., 82.

13. Ibid., 112.

14. Ruth Myers, Warren Myers, *31 Days of Praise* (Sisters, Oregon; Multnomah Publishers, Inc., 1994), 40–41.